Ready-to-Go Lessons

Grade 3

About This Book

Your friends at *The Mailbox®* have done it again! We've combined four previously published books from the Lifesaver Lessons® series for Grade 3 *(Language Arts, Math, Science,* and *Social Studies)* into one comprehensive edition. This new compilation—*Ready-to-Go Lessons, Grade 3*—offers everything you need in one book to supplement all four curriculum areas for your grade level.

What Are Ready-to-Go Lessons?

Just as the name implies, this book includes well-planned, easy-to-implement, curriculum-based lessons that are ready to go in minutes. Each lesson contains a complete materials list, step-by-step instructions, a reproducible activity or pattern, and several extension activities.

How Do I Use a Ready-to-Go Lesson?

Each lesson is designed to decrease your preparation time and increase the amount of quality teaching time with your students. These lessons are great for introducing or reinforcing language arts, math, science, and social studies concepts. They'll even come in handy if you're planning for a substitute, as each lesson is planned and written for you and the materials can be easily gathered in advance. After completing each lesson as described, try one or more of the fun-filled extension activities that are included with each lesson.

What Materials Will I Need?

We've tried to make each lesson as easy to implement as possible, so most of the materials can be easily found right in your classroom. Be sure to read each materials list prior to the activity, as some supplies might need to be gathered from your school library or supply room.

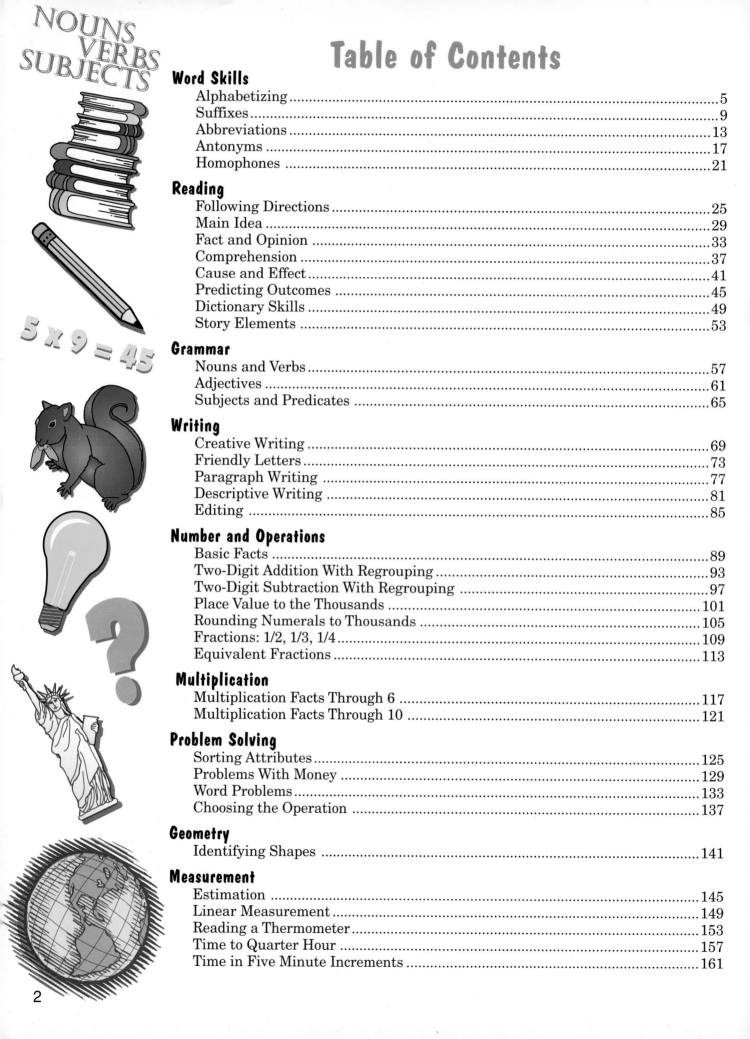

Table of Contents

Word Skills

Alphabetizing 5
Suffixes 9
Abbreviations 13
Antonyms 17
Homophones 21

Reading

Following Directions 25
Main Idea 29
Fact and Opinion 33
Comprehension 37
Cause and Effect 41
Predicting Outcomes 45
Dictionary Skills 49
Story Elements 53

Grammar

Nouns and Verbs 57
Adjectives 61
Subjects and Predicates 65

Writing

Creative Writing 69
Friendly Letters 73
Paragraph Writing 77
Descriptive Writing 81
Editing 85

Number and Operations

Basic Facts 89
Two-Digit Addition With Regrouping 93
Two-Digit Subtraction With Regrouping 97
Place Value to the Thousands 101
Rounding Numerals to Thousands 105
Fractions: 1/2, 1/3, 1/4 109
Equivalent Fractions 113

Multiplication

Multiplication Facts Through 6 117
Multiplication Facts Through 10 121

Problem Solving

Sorting Attributes 125
Problems With Money 129
Word Problems 133
Choosing the Operation 137

Geometry

Identifying Shapes 141

Measurement

Estimation 145
Linear Measurement 149
Reading a Thermometer 153
Time to Quarter Hour 157
Time in Five Minute Increments 161

Graphing

Bar Graphs 165
Line Graphs 169
Circle Graphs 173

Life Science

Life Cycles 177
Animal Adaptations 181
Vertebrates 185
Animal Facts 189

Physical Science

States of Matter 193
Changes in Matter 197
Simple Machines 201
Light 205
Sources of Sounds 209
Sources of Heat 213

Earth Science

Planet Order 217
Researching Planets 221
Earth's Habitats 225
Earth's Layers 229
Rocks 233
Signs of Erosion 237

Communities

Urban, Suburban, and Rural Settings 241
The Interdependence of Individuals 245
Natural Resources of the Community 249

Government and Citizenship

Community Laws 253
Rights and Responsibilities of Citizens 257
Democratic Decision Making 261
U.S. Monuments and Landforms 265
Local, State, and National Leaders 269

Map Skills

Cardinal and Intermediate Directions 273
Grids 277
Product Maps 281
Geographic Terms 285
Continents and Oceans 289
Using a Scale 293

Economics

Community Services 297
Goods and Services 301
Specialization and Division of Labor 305
A Producer Is a Consumer 309

Reproducibles 313

Answer Keys 317

3

From Your Friends at The MAILBOX®

Ready-to-Go Lessons

Grade 3

Managing Editor: Scott Lyons
Contributing Writers: Brenda Dunlap, Amy Erickson, Kimberly Fields, Ellen Fortson, Heather Graley, Cynthia Holcomb, Nicole Iacovazzi, Martha Kelly, Kathleen N. Kopp, Susan Kotchman, Mary Ann Lewis, Linda Manwiller, Geoffrey Mihalenko, Patricia Pecuch, Julie Plowman, Stacie Stone Smith, Stephanie Willett-Smith, Valerie Wood Smith, Cheryl Stickney, Laura Wagner, Jan Wittstrom
Copy Editors: Sylvan Allen, Karen Brewer Grossman, Karen L. Huffman, Amy Kirtley-Hill, Debbie Shoffner
Cover Artist: Nick Greenwood
Art Coordinator: Rebecca Saunders
Artists: Pam Crane, Theresa Lewis Goode, Nick Greenwood, Clevell Harris, Ivy L. Koonce, Sheila Krill, Clint Moore, Greg D. Rieves, Rebecca Saunders, Barry Slate, Stuart Smith, Donna K. Teal
Typesetters: Lynette Dickerson, Mark Rainey

President, The Mailbox Book Company™: Joseph C. Bucci
Director of Book Planning and Development: Chris Poindexter
Book Development Managers: Elizabeth H. Lindsay, Thad McLaurin, Susan Walker
Curriculum Director: Karen P. Shelton
Traffic Manager: Lisa K. Pitts
Librarian: Dorothy C. McKinney
Editorial and Freelance Management: Karen A. Brudnak
Editorial Training: Irving P. Crump
Editorial Assistants: Terrie Head, Hope Rodgers, Jan E. Witcher

www.themailbox.com

©2002 by THE EDUCATION CENTER, INC.
All rights reserved.
ISBN #1-56234-521-4

Manufactured in the United States
10 9 8 7 6 5 4 3 2

A "Bee" C

Your students will be all a-buzz with this honey of a lesson to reinforce alphabetizing skills.

Skill: Alphabetizing to the third letter

Estimated Lesson Time: 30 minutes

Teacher Preparation:
Duplicate page 7 for each student.

Materials:
1 copy of page 7 per student

fact	crab	brain
fall	creek	bread
fame	crib	brick
favor	crown	broom
fawn	crumb	brunch

Introducing The Lesson:

Ask students to think of words that begin with the letter *b*. List the responses on the board and have students arrange the words in alphabetical order. Then tell students that they will "bee" on a mission to get some hives in order.

Steps:

1. Review rules for alphabetizing to the third letter.

2. Distribute a copy of page 7 to each student.

3. Pair students together to check their answers.

4. Challenge students to complete the Bonus Box activity.

baby	best	block	brown
back	big	blue	brush
ball	bike	boat	bump
bat	bill	boss	bunch
beach	bird	bow	bus
bell	black	brave	buzz
bench	blend	bright	

A "Bee" C

Arrange the words buzzing around each bee in alphabetical order.
Write the words in ABC order on the hives.

How To Extend The Lesson:

- Have students make an alphabetized list of foods on the daily lunch menu.

- Divide the class into two groups and have each group alphabetize the titles of their library books.

- Ask each student to choose a crayon from his box; then have students line up in alphabetical order according to the color names of their crayons.

- List the names of five stores on the board. Have students work in pairs to look up the store names in the phone book.

- Have students brainstorm a list of items that contain alphabetized information, or places where alphabetical order is used to organize materials.

- Program copies of the patterns below with vocabulary words. Place the patterns in a center. Encourage each student to visit the center and arrange the words in alphabetical order.

Patterns

©The Education Center, Inc.   ©The Education Center, Inc.

In Search Of Suffixes

Turn your students into supersleuths with this activity to track down suffixes!

Skill: Recognizing suffixes

Estimated Lesson Time: 40 minutes

Teacher Preparation:
1. Duplicate page 11 for each student.
2. Gather several newspapers, enough for each student to have her own section.

Materials:
1 copy of page 11 per student
newspapers
scissors
glue

Background Information:
A *suffix* is an affix added to the end of a word or stem, forming a new word or an inflectional ending.

Suffix	Meaning
-able, -ible	able to, capable of
-ance, -ence, -ancy, -ency	quality, act, or condition
-ar, -er, -or	one who does something
-er, -est	superlative adjective
-ful	full of
-fy	to form into or become
-hood	state of being, membership in a group
-ing	gerund form of a verb, can form nouns from verbs
-ion, -sion, -tion	act, process, or condition
-ish	nationality, having likeness to
-ive	having the quality of, tending to
-less	without
-like	similar to
-ly	in a certain manner
-ment	result of, action or process
-ness	manner or state of being
-ward	toward, in the direction of
-wise	way, direction
-y, -ey	quality or state of

Introducing The Lesson:

Tell your detectives that they are going to go on a newspaper scavenger hunt to search for certain suffixes. Review the definitions of suffixes, focusing on *-ful, -less, -ing, -ly,* and *-ment*. Explain that each student is to look in the newspaper for words containing those suffixes. When a word is found, the student cuts and pastes it under the appropriate column on page 11.

Steps:

1. Distribute a copy of page 11 to each student.

2. Provide each student with newspapers, scissors, and glue.

3. Instruct students to search through the newspapers for words that contain the suffixes shown at the top of page 11.

4. Tell students to cut and paste the identified suffixes in the appropriate columns on page 11.

5. Provide students with a given amount of time to complete the activity. Then challenge them to complete the Bonus Box activity.

In Search Of…Suffixes

Look through newspapers for words that contain the suffixes shown below. Cut and paste each word in the correct column.

- -ful
- -less
- -ing
- -ly
- -ment

In The News **SECTION C**

SUFFIXES

-ful	-less	-ing	-ly	-ment

City Council Votes To Ration Ice Cream **Local**

Bonus Box: On the back of the page, write the definition of one word in each column.

How To Extend The Lesson:

- Have a pair of students read a storybook. Ask them to make a list of suffixes found in the story.

- Assign each student a suffix. Challenge him to list ten words that contain the suffix.

- Make a suffix dictionary. Have each student write a suffix, its meaning, and a sentence containing the word on a sheet of paper. Alphabetize the pages; then compile them into a class dictionary.

- Write a root word on the board. Challenge each student to list as many suffixes as possible that can be added to the word.

- Focus on one suffix each day. Ask students to be on the lookout for words containing the suffix, and keep a list of their discoveries on the board.

Today's suffix: -est

oldest	fastest
slowest	coldest
hardest	greatest
smallest	brightest
shortest	boldest
tallest	loudest

Just What The Doctor Ordered!

This prescription for abbreviations will provide students with a healthy dose of practice.

Skill: Identifying abbreviations

Estimated Lesson Time: 30 minutes

Teacher Preparation:
1. Duplicate page 15 for each student.
2. Gather several student dictionaries.

Materials:
1 copy of page 15 per student
several student dictionaries

Teacher Reference:

a.m.	before noon	Mt.	Mountain
appt.	appointment	p.m.	after noon
apt.	apartment	pg.	page
Ave.	Avenue	vocab.	vocabulary
Blvd.	Boulevard	ASAP	as soon as possible
Co.	Company	ID	identification
dept.	department	IOU	I owe you
Dr.	Doctor	MPH	miles per hour
Hwy.	Highway	TV	television
Mr.	Title for a man	VIP	very important person
Mrs.	Title for a married woman		

Introducing The Lesson:

Tell students that you are very tired today and you don't have much energy to write. On the board, write this sentence: "On Mon. we will read pg. 14 and answer the 2nd question." Ask students to identify the words that saved you energy in your writing.

Steps:

1. Have volunteers circle each abbreviation and then write the long form of each word.

2. Brainstorm with students a list of words that can be abbreviated. Record the words and the abbreviated spellings on the board.

3. Distribute a copy of page 15 to each student. Provide dictionaries for student reference.

4. Challenge students to complete the Bonus Box activity.

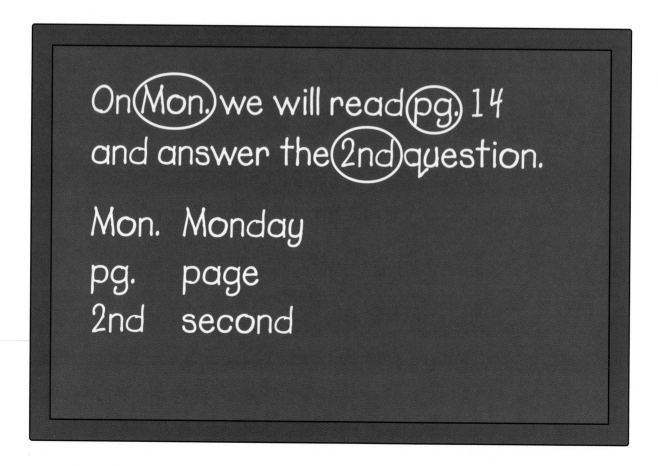

Just What The Doctor Ordered!

Read the paragraph and circle each abbreviation.
Then write the spelling of each abbreviated word.

   Last night I visited with Dr. Frederick Fungus, Jr., the most famous surgeon in the U.S.A. He told me of a patient he treated last Tues. afternoon. Since Jan. 1st, the patient had been having trouble with his hearing. After examining the patient, Frederick found the problem. He rushed the man to the hospital E.R. on the corner of Main St. and Pine Rd., where he pulled a meatball from the man's ear. The man was very relieved. It was the 3rd time it had happened to him. He says it happens every time he falls asleep while eating spaghetti.

abbreviation   complete spelling of word

1._____   _____

2._____   _____

3._____   _____

4._____   _____

5._____   _____

6._____   _____

7._____   _____

8._____   _____

9._____   _____

10._____   _____

Bonus Box: Create an abbreviation for the name of each person in your family.

How To Extend The Lesson:

- Have students look through the telephone book to find abbreviations. Challenge them to find and list at least ten.

- List some common abbreviated terms such as FBI, NBA, FYI, ASAP, and UFO. Have students guess what the acronyms stand for before you explain the meanings.

- Have students learn the abbreviations for the states. Introduce three or four abbreviations each day. Then quiz students in a spelling-bee-type contest to see who can identify the most states by their abbreviations.

- Tell each student to write a sentence. Then have him try to abbreviate several words in the sentence. Call on students to write their abbreviated sentences on the board for the class to try to decipher.

State	Abbr.	State	Abbr.	State	Abbr.
Alabama	AL	Kentucky	KY	North Dakota	ND
Alaska	AK	Louisiana	LA	Ohio	OH
Arizona	AZ	Maine	ME	Oklahoma	OK
Arkansas	AR	Maryland	MD	Oregon	OR
California	CA	Massachusetts	MA	Pennsylvania	PA
Colorado	CO	Michigan	MI	Rhode Island	RI
Connecticut	CT	Minnesota	MN	South Carolina	SC
Delaware	DE	Mississippi	MS	South Dakota	SD
District of Columbia	DC	Missouri	MO	Tennessee	TN
Florida	FL	Montana	MT	Texas	TX
Georgia	GA	Nebraska	NE	Utah	UT
Hawaii	HI	Nevada	NV	Vermont	VT
Idaho	ID	New Hampshire	NH	Virginia	VA
Illinois	IL	New Jersey	NJ	Washington	WA
Indiana	IN	New Mexico	NM	West Virginia	WV
Iowa	IA	New York	NY	Wisconsin	WI
Kansas	KS	North Carolina	NC	Wyoming	WY

Amazing Antonyms

Explore opposite words with this activity that promotes student individuality.

Skill: Using antonyms

Estimated Lesson Time: 30 minutes

Teacher Preparation:
1. Duplicate a copy of page 19 for each student.
2. Program pairs of index cards with opposite words. Prepare enough cards so that each student will have one.

Materials:
1 copy of page 19 per student
index cards programmed with antonyms

Background Information:
Antonyms are words with opposite meanings.

Teacher Reference:

above—below	crooked—straight	false—true	polite—rude
add—subtract	cry—laugh	forget—remember	poor—rich
alike—different	dangerous—safe	found—lost	right—wrong
asleep—awake	day—night	frown—smile	rough—smooth
backward—forward	deep—shallow	generous—selfish	save—spend
beautiful—ugly	destroy—repair	hard—soft	short—tall
begin—finish	difficult—easy	left—right	sour—sweet
believe—doubt	dry—wet	lose—win	tame—wild
big—small	early—late	noisy—quiet	terrible—wonderful
buy—sell	enemy—friend	over—under	whisper—yell
clean—dirty	fast—slow	play—work	

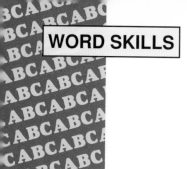
Introducing The Lesson:

Begin this activity with a mixed-up matching game. Tell students that instead of playing a game where they find a matching pair of cards, they are to find cards that don't match; in fact, they must find cards that are complete opposites!

Steps:

1. Distribute an index card to each student. Instruct each student to find the person holding a card programmed with the opposite meaning from the word on his card. When students have paired up, have each pair announce the words on their cards. Explain that the term for an opposite word is *antonym*.

2. Distribute a copy of page 19 to each student.

3. Have each student complete the reproducible; then share the possible answers in a class discussion.

4. Challenge students to complete the Bonus Box activity.

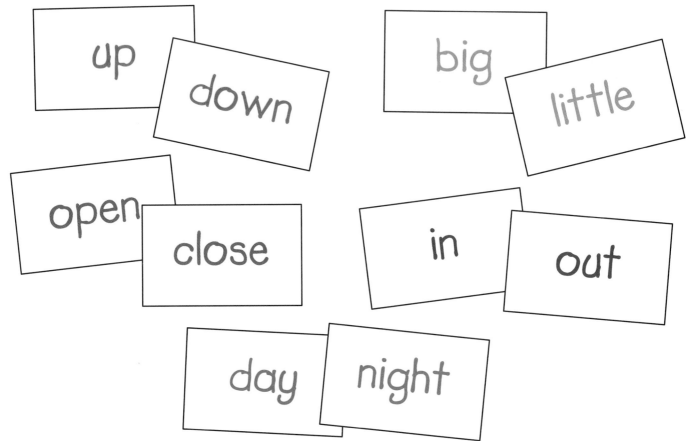

Name _____

Amazing Antonyms

Complete each sentence with words that make the sentence true.

1. A _____ is cold, but a _____ is hot.

2. We see the _____ in the day, and the _____ at night.

3. A _____ is small, but a _____ is large.

4. _____ makes me happy, but _____ makes me sad.

5. A _____ is smooth, and a _____ is rough.

6. _____ is short, but _____ is tall.

7. I think _____ tastes good, and _____ tastes bad.

8. I like _____ in the summer, and _____ in the winter.

9. At my house, the _____ is empty, but the _____ is full.

10. A _____ is very slow, but a _____ is very fast.

Bonus Box: Underline the antonyms in each sentence.

©The Education Center, Inc. • *Ready-to-Go Lessons* • TEC1116

How To Extend The Lesson:

- Write a character sketch on the board with a list of characteristics such as *tall, thin, kind, forgetful, likes to sing, runs quickly,* and *has an elephant.* Ask each student to write a description of a character who is the complete opposite of the one outlined on the board. Then have each student write a story using the two opposite characters.

- Have each student submit a paper with a paragraph telling about the best thing that has happened to him in third grade, and a paragraph telling about his worst third-grade experience. Compile student writing in a book titled "The Best And Worst Of Third Grade."

- Create an antonym list for several categories. Have students brainstorm animals that are considered opposites (such as a lion and a lamb, and a tortoise and a hare), time periods that are opposites (such as day and night, summer and winter, and a.m. and p.m.) and opposite words for these categories: action words, emotions, descriptions, and weather.

- Share these stories that have opposite themes with your students:
  —*Becca Backward, Becca Frontward: A Book Of Concept Pairs* by Bruce McMillan (Lothrop, Lee & Shepard; 1986)
  —*Fast-Slow, High-Low* by Peter Spier (Doubleday, 1988)
  —*Jethro And Joel Were A Troll* by Bill Peet (Houghton Mifflin Company, 1990)
  —*Red Cat, White Cat* by Peter Mandel (Henry Holt and Company, Inc.; 1994)
  —*Traffic: A Book Of Opposites* by Betsy Maestro and Giulio Maestro (Crown Books For Young Readers, 1991)

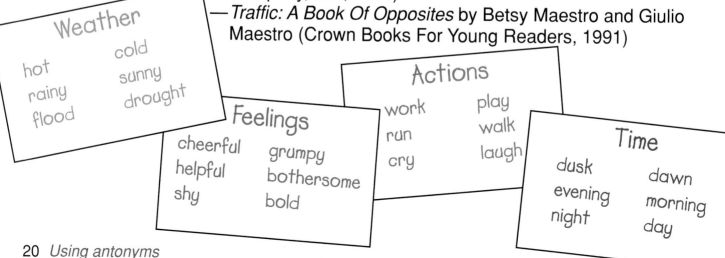

Weather
hot   cold
rainy   sunny
flood   drought

Feelings
cheerful   grumpy
helpful   bothersome
shy   bold

Actions
work   play
run   walk
cry   laugh

Time
dusk   dawn
evening   morning
night   day

Two Scoops

Here's a tasty approach to reviewing homophone word pairs.

Skill: Discovering homophones

Estimated Lesson Time: 30 minutes

Teacher Preparation:
Duplicate page 23 for each student.

Materials:
1 copy of page 23 per student

Teacher Reference:

ate—eight	knight—night	sale—sail
be—bee	knot—not	sea—see
bear—bare	know—no	sew—so
blew—blue	knows—nose	some—sum
buy—by—bye	made—maid	son—sun
cents—scents—sense	male—mail	tail—tale
deer—dear	meat—meet—mete	there—their—they're
eye—I—aye	one—won	through—threw
hair—hare	pair—pear—pare	to—too—two
hear—here	plane—plain	way—weigh
hole—whole	principal—principle	week—weak
hour—our	red—read	would—wood
knew—new—gnu	road—rode	write—right—rite

Introducing The Lesson:

Tell students to close their eyes and picture an image for the sentence you are going to say out loud. When students have closed their eyes, say, "I ate one bowl of ice cream for breakfast." Have students open their eyes and describe the images they saw. Then write on the board "Eye eight won bowl of ice cream four breakfast." Ask students to proofread the sentence.

Steps:

1. Have student volunteers circle the words that are misspelled in the sentence.

2. Ask students to help you spell the correct form of each circled word. Discuss the word meanings of each homophone pair.

3. Distribute page 23 to each student.

4. Provide time for students to complete the homophone activity.

5. Challenge students to complete the Bonus Box activity.

Name _____

Two Scoops

Find the homonym pairs from the flavor list.
Write the pairs on the matching ice-cream cones.
Circle the word that is pictured on each cone.

Flavors
write
some
son
bare
deer
flour
would
knows
right
hair
sum
dear
flower
nose
hare
wood
sun
bear

1.

$$\frac{3}{7} = 4$$

2.

3.

4.

5.

6.

7.

8.

9.

Bonus Box: Choose three homonym pairs. Write the meaning for each of the words on the back of this page.

How To Extend The Lesson:

- Place a supply of ice-cream scoop cutouts at a learning center. (See the patterns below.) Encourage students to think of homophone pairs and write each word of the pair on a scoop. Glue the scoops atop a cone-shaped cutout and staple the resulting ice-cream cone to a bulletin-board display.

- Use the ice-cream scoop patterns below to create a class supply of vocabulary cards. Program each scoop with the definition of one word in a homophone pair. Distribute a programmed scoop to each student. The student reads the definition and writes the word it defines on the back of the scoop. He then finds a student with a word that makes a homophone pair with his word. Have each student pair read their words and definitions to the class; then store the programmed scoops in a center for additional review.

- Initiate some wordplay into the classroom with this collection of books by Fred Gwynne. *A Little Pigeon Toad*, *A Chocolate Moose For Dinner*, and *The King Who Rained* (Simon and Schuster Children's Books, 1988) are full of humorous homophones, delightful double meanings, and clever illustrations. After sharing the books with your class, have students try their hands at creating plays on words.

Patterns

Focus On Following Directions

Students will learn the value of following directions with this activity that sharpens attention to detail.

Skill: Following written directions

Estimated Lesson Time: 20 minutes

Teacher Preparation:
Duplicate page 27 for each student.

Materials:
1 copy of page 27 per student

Following Directions Are Important When:

- Preparing a recipe
- Following safety procedures
- Assembling toys and other items
- Completing school assignments
- Taking medication
- Reading an instruction sheet
- Playing a game

Introducing The Lesson:

Ask students to brainstorm times when it is important to follow directions. Announce to your class that you have an important document that will assess each student's ability to follow written directions. The directions are not hard, but students will need to read carefully. As a pretest exercise, you will call out several directions, Simon Says style, to help students focus on paying attention to details.

Steps:

1. Call out several Simon Says directions, using instructions such as "Get out a pencil," "Put your feet flat on the floor," "Sit up straight," and "Read the directions on the upcoming paper carefully."

2. Distribute a copy of page 27 to each student. Remind students that the directions will be easy to follow, but should be read carefully.

3. Challenge students to complete the Bonus Box activity.

Simon says,
"Get out a pencil."

Simon says,
"Put your feet flat on the floor."

Stretch your arms
above your head.

Simon says,
"Sit up straight."

Wave your pencil in the air.

Simon says,
"Read the directions on the
upcoming paper carefully."

Can You Follow Directions?

Read carefully to follow the directions on the page.

1. Read this entire list of directions before completing them.

2. Write your name at the top of the paper.

3. Put a star by your name at the top of the paper.

4. Circle the third word in this sentence.

5. Underline the last word in this sentence.

6. Color in all the *O*s in this sentence.

7. Cross out the second word in this sentence.

8. Draw a box around the shortest word in this sentence.

9. Turn the paper over and write your last name three times.

10. Now that you have finished reading all the directions, complete only number two. Then try the Bonus Box activity.

Bonus Box: On the back of this paper, make a list of jobs where it is not important to follow directions.

How To Extend The Lesson:

- Provide practice with listening skills by calling out a list of directions for students to follow. Instruct each student to complete such directions as writing her name in the upper left corner of her paper, writing the date in the lower left corner, drawing a tree in the center of the paper, and other simple instructions.

- Emphasize the importance of giving directions as well as following them. Have each student write a list of directions for preparing an easy snack, such as peanut butter and crackers. After he completes his list, let each student prepare the snack according to his directions. Help the student revise his directions if any key information was left out.

- Play a game of Simon Says to sharpen listening skills. Incorporate content review into the directions, such as "Simon says to show 18 minus 13 fingers," or "Simon says to face north."

- Combine listening skills and following directions with math practice. Call out a series of numbers and operations for students to write down. (For example, "Three plus five times two minus four.") Allow time for students to work the problem; then award a token for each correct response.

Tokens

Give The Main Idea A Hand!

Students will learn to state the main idea of any story with this helping hand!

Skill: Determining the main idea

Estimated Lesson Time: 30 minutes

Teacher Preparation:
1. Duplicate page 31 for each student.
2. Select a story the class has read together.

Materials:
1 copy of page 31 per student
1 story the class has read together

When? Where?
What?
Why?
Who?

Introducing The Lesson:

Announce to students that you have a piece of special equipment to help locate the main idea of any story. Tell them that you are going to show them the equipment and demonstrate the proper technique for using it. Then you will allow each student to practice using the equipment to locate the main idea of a story.

Steps:

1. Make a great fanfare of holding up your hand, showing students the front and back, and then drawing the outline of a hand on the board.

2. Tell students that to use the special equipment (the hand) they must remember to use each and every part (point to the fingers on the drawing). Each part will reveal an important piece of the main-idea statement.

3. Label the fingers on the hand diagram as follows: "when," "where," "who," "what," and "why." Tell students that when all of the pieces are put together, the main-idea statement is revealed.

4. Lead your students through a practice story such as *Little Red Riding Hood.* Have students volunteer information for the hand diagram while you record the answers on the corresponding finger:
   When: *Once upon a time*
   Where: *in the woods*
   Who: *a little girl*
   What: *met a tricky wolf*
   Why: *because she was taking a shortcut to her grandmother's house.*

5. Demonstrate how to put the information together to write a main-idea statement: *Once upon a time, a little girl met a tricky wolf in the woods as she was going to her grandmother's house.*

6. Distribute a copy of page 31 to each student. Have students complete it using a story the whole class has read.

7. Challenge students to complete the Bonus Box activity.

Give The Main Idea A Hand!

Complete the diagram by filling in the information on each finger.
Use the information to write a main-idea statement.

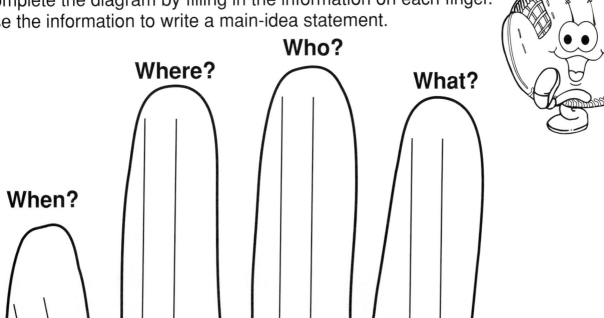

Where?

Who?

What?

When?

Why?

Now write your main-idea statement.

_____

_____

_____

_____

_____

_____

Bonus Box: On the back of this paper, illustrate your main-idea statement.

How To Extend The Lesson:

• Use the reproducible as a prewriting tool for creative-writing assignments. Each student brainstorms ideas for a story by developing the main idea first. After using the reproducible to outline the story's main idea, the student writes his creative tale.

• Reinforce story elements by reviewing a completed reproducible with your class. Ask students to find the information that describes the character, setting, and plot.

• Have students read copies of a short newspaper article and fill out the reproducible to state the main idea. Ask each student to list additional details of the article on a separate piece of paper. Share the responses to compare the main idea to supporting details.

• Use the reproducible as a follow-up to a video or play performance.

• Emphasize the main idea in a paragraph using the hand diagram. Draw the shape of the hand on the board and ask students to complete it with information from a paragraph they have read together.

Award

YOU DESERVE A HAND FOR FINDING THE MAIN IDEA!

Name _____

©The Education Center, Inc. • *Ready-to-Go Lessons* • TEC1116

Fairy-Tale Facts & Opinions

When using a fairy tale to reinforce facts and opinions, students will learn happily ever after!

Skill: Studying facts and opinions

Estimated Lesson Time: 35 minutes

Teacher Preparation:

1. Duplicate the reproducible on page 35 for each student.
2. Select a fairy tale to read aloud to the class.

Materials:

1 copy of page 35 per student
1 fairy tale

Facts	Opinions
Red is a girl.	Red is careless.
The pig has a hammer.	Pigs are hard workers.
The wolf has big teeth.	The wolf is up to no good.

Introducing The Lesson:

Help students discern the difference between facts and opinions. Record the responses on the board. Ask them to think of fact and opinion statements about themselves.

Steps:

1. Discuss with students the difference between the facts and the opinions.

2. Explain to your students that they are going to hear a fairy tale, and each student will choose a character from the story for a fact and opinion activity.

3. Read a fairy tale aloud to the class.

4. Provide each student with a copy of page 35.

5. Ask each student to choose a character and design a face for the character.

6. Have students write facts and opinions about that character.

7. Challenge students to complete the Bonus Box activity.

Facts	Opinions
I have blue eyes.	My blue eyes are pretty.
I am eight years old.	Eight-year-olds are noisy.
I have freckles.	Freckles are attractive.
I have two brothers.	My brothers are funny.

Fairy-Tale Facts & Opinions

Choose a character from the fairy tale you've read.
Write the character's name and the story title below.
Draw the character's face inside the oval shape.
Then list five facts and five opinions about the character.

_____ Title

_____ Character

Facts About Me

1. _____

2. _____

3. _____

4. _____

5. _____

Opinions About Me

1. _____

2. _____

3. _____

4. _____

5. _____

Bonus Box: Read your facts and opinions about this character. Decide if you'd want to be friends with this character. Write the reasons on the back of the page.

How To Extend The Lesson:

- Ask each student to write five facts and five opinions about himself. Post the resulting lists anonymously and have students attempt to match each list to the person who wrote it.

- Write the names of several famous persons on separate index cards. Tell each student to select a card and ask her to find as many facts and opinions as she can about the famous person.

- Provide each student with a card labeled "fact" and a card labeled "opinion." (See the patterns below.) Make several statements about a story or subject, and ask each student to hold up the appropriate card as the statement is given.

It's a
FACT!

It can be proven.

It's an
OPINION!

It is a belief or judgment.

Catch A Question

Students use comprehension skills to toss around some great ideas in this small-group reading activity.

Skill: Developing reading comprehension

Estimated Lesson Time: 40 minutes

Teacher Preparation:

1. Duplicate page 39 for each student.
2. Prepare six questions about a story the whole class has read.
3. Write each question on a piece of 8 1/2" by 11" paper, and number each question.

Materials:

1 copy of page 39 per student
6 sheets of 8 1/2" by 11" paper, each programmed with a question

1. Who was the main character?
2. What problem or challenge did the character face?

3. Who are three minor characters in the story?
4. How did the ending affect the main character?

5. How was the setting important to the story?
6. Could this story take place in a different time period?

Introducing The Lesson:

Tell students that they are going to work in groups to answer questions about a story they have read. There is an unusual catch to the activity—when each group is through with their question, they toss it to another group, and then catch a new question to answer.

Steps:

1. Distribute a copy of page 39 to each student.

2. Divide students into six groups.

3. Distribute a question to each group and instruct each student to write the group's answer by the corresponding number on the reproducible.

4. After each group has answered the question, give a signal for a member from each group to crumple the paper with the question into a ball and toss it to another group.

5. Each group unfolds the new question and answers it. Repeat the procedure until all six questions have been answered by each group.

6. Challenge students to complete the Bonus Box activity.

Who was the main character?

Catch A Question

Discuss each question with the members of your group.
Write the answer in a complete sentence beside the correct number.

Title Of Story: _____

1. _____ .

   _____ .

2. _____ .

   _____ .

3. _____ .

   _____ .

4. _____ .

   _____ .

5. _____ .

   _____ .

6. _____ .

   _____ .

Bonus Box: On the back of this page, tell three things about your favorite character in the story.

How To Extend The Lesson:

- Have students write interview questions to ask a character in the story. Select students to role-play the characters during the interviews.

- Ask each group to write a sequel to the story. Have them illustrate the characters to show how they have changed or grown up since the original story.

- Place students into groups to discuss how the story would be different if the time or place of the story were different. Then have each group rewrite the story using a new setting. Share the new stories with the class.

- Have students write the questions for "Catch A Question" when they have finished reading a new story. Provide copies of the form below for students to use in listing their questions.

Name _____

Did you catch the answer to these questions?

1. _____

_____ ?

2. _____

_____ ?

3. _____

_____ ?

©The Education Center, Inc. • *Ready-to-Go Lessons* • TEC1116

Cause-And-Effect Grab Bag

There's no question about it…this bag of tricks will help your students zero in on cause-and-effect situations.

Skill: Identifying cause and effect

Estimated Lesson Time: 35 minutes

Teacher Preparation:

1. Duplicate the reproducible on page 43 for each student.
2. Select a story to read aloud to the class.

Materials:

1 copy of page 43 per student
1 story to read aloud
1 paper bag

It started to rain.

We ran to find shelter.

It was Mary's birthday.

We baked her a cake.

CAUSE

EFFECT

We heard the bell.

We sat down in our seats.

Introducing The Lesson:

Ask students to raise their hands if they have a favorite story. When several students raise their hands, ask them *why* they are holding up their hands. Confirm that the reason is that they are responding to a question. The teacher asked a question, which *caused* students to respond. The *effect* was that the students held up their hands. Instruct students to look for cause-and-effect situations in the upcoming story.

Steps:

1. Select a story and read it aloud to the students, or have the students read the story together.

2. Distribute a copy of page 43 to each student.

3. Have students cut the paper on the dotted lines and fold it in half once, then in half again.

4. Ask each student to write a question asking *why* something happened in the story on the outside of the paper. The student then writes the answer to the question on the inside of the folded paper.

5. Tell each student to put his question inside the paper bag.

6. Have a student select a question and read it to the class. The student with the correct answer may choose the next question to read aloud.

7. Challenge students to complete the Bonus Box activity after all the questions have been selected and answered.

Question Grab Bag

After reading a story, write a "why" question and its correct
   answer in the appropriate spaces below.
Cut along the dotted lines.
Fold the paper in half once, then in half again.
Put your question and answer inside the paper bag.

Answer:

Question:

Bonus Box: Use your imagination! Draw illustrations for your question and answer.

How To Extend The Lesson:

- Challenge your students to write sequels to the story. Encourage students to read their stories to the class. Ask students to identify a cause-and-effect situation in each sequel.

- Tell each student to fold a piece of paper in half. Have him draw an event that happened in the story on one side and draw its effect on the other side.

- Create a cause-and-effect Concentration game. Write or draw a cause and its effect on separate index cards. Make several sets of cards. To play, student partners place the cards facedown and take turns selecting two cards at a time in search of a corresponding set.

Ribsy did not come home.

Henry put an ad in the paper.

LOST DOG

A dog that shakes hands with its left paw.

What A Story!

Students combine prediction skills with imagination in this creative-writing activity.

Skill: Predicting outcomes

Estimated Lesson Time: 45 minutes

Teacher Preparation:
Duplicate page 47 for each student.

Materials:
1 copy of page 47 per student

characters:

- crab
- ladybug
- ballerina
- raccoon
- wrestler
- outlaw
- hippo

settings:

- a beach
- a bus
- a restaurant
- the Statue of Liberty
- the jungle
- the post office
- a candy store
- a pay phone

situations:

- A rainstorm begins.
- A character explains why he is late for school.
- A character picks up the wrong sack at the drug-store.
- A character makes a cake with salt instead of sugar.
- A character gets on the wrong plane.
- A character is given a surprise party.

Introducing The Lesson:

Ask students to imagine what might happen if someone brought a pet snake for show-and-tell, and it got loose in the classroom. Have students volunteer their ideas. Tell students that they have just made *predictions* about what could happen. Tell students that they will be making predictions for several different story situations.

Steps:

1. Distribute a copy of page 47 to each student.

2. Provide time for students to make story predictions.

3. Challenge students to complete the Bonus Box activity.

Who would be afraid of the snake?

What could the snake eat?

Where would the snake try to hide?

When did someone notice it was missing?

Why did the snake get loose?

Name _____

What A Story!

Read each section of story information.
Tell what might happen in the story.

Characters: a grandmother and a gorilla
Setting: the grocery store
Situation: Grandmother has lost her glasses and
   is having trouble reading her shopping list.
What happens? _____

_____

_____

_____

_____

Characters: a snake and a turtle
Setting: a movie theater
Situation: The snake and the turtle are having trouble seeing the movie screen.
What happens? _____

_____

_____

_____

_____

Characters: a cowboy and an opera singer
Setting: a doughnut shop
Situation: The two characters both want the last jelly doughnut.
What happens? _____

_____

_____

_____

_____

Characters: a boy and a kangaroo
Setting: a park
Situation: The boy wants to take the kangaroo home as a pet.
What happens? _____

_____

_____

_____

_____

Bonus Box: Draw a picture to go with each story idea.

How To Extend The Lesson:

- Have student volunteers read their story ideas to the class. Discuss stories with similar ideas. Have students surmise why some stories' ideas contain similar elements.

- Create a writing center with a supply of writing paper and three containers labeled "characters," "settings," and "situations." Fill each container with a supply of index cards programmed with appropriate story information. A student visits the center to draw a card from each container. After reading the information, the student writes a story idea using details from the cards. Provide time for students to share their work with the class.

- Begin reading a story to the class, stopping at a crucial part of the story. Have each student write a few sentences telling what he predicts will happen. Allow student volunteers to share their predictions with the class before you finish reading the story.

- Have students create ideas for characters, settings, and situations. Ask each student to write the information on a copy of the form below, then trade papers with a classmate and write a story idea using the classmate's information. Students then trade papers back to share their ideas with each other.

What could happen with:		
Characters	**Setting**	**Situation**

Dictionary Safari

Lead your students into the deepest, darkest corners of the dictionary to track down more than just definitions.

Skill: Using a dictionary

Estimated Lesson Time: 45 minutes

Teacher Preparation:

1. Duplicate page 51 for each student.
2. Provide a dictionary for each student.

Materials:

1 copy of page 51 per student
1 dictionary per student

safari   sail

sa • fa' • ri \ sə- 'fär -ē \ *n* 1. the caravan and equipment of a hunting expedition 2. journey, expedition

Introducing The Lesson:

Tell students that they are going to track down some wild, ferocious words. After locating each word, students will capture its meaning on paper and then bag it as a trophy definition.

Steps:

1. Review the term *guide words* and how to use them.

2. Ask students to brainstorm words they consider wild and ferocious, either by the way they sound or by their definitions. List the responses on the board.

3. Distribute a copy of page 51 and a dictionary to each student. Instruct each student to choose two words from the list to use in completing the reproducible.

4. Challenge students to complete the Bonus Box activity.

terrible	bizarre	shocking
fierce	wacky	sensational
reckless	goofy	dreadful
fantastic	strange	incredible
unbelievable	outrageous	gigantic
berserk	disgraceful	tough
frenzy	grizzly	

Dictionary Safari

List the two words you are going to track down.
Then complete the information about each word to capture it on paper.

Word One _____

1. Write the word by syllables. Capitalize the accented syllable. _____

2. How many definitions does the word have? _____

3. Write the first definition. _____

_____

4. What part of speech is the word? _____

5. What are the guide words on the page? _____ and _____

Word Two _____

1. Write the word by syllables. Capitalize the accented syllable. _____

2. How many definitions does the word have? _____

3. Write the first definition. _____

_____

4. What part of speech is the word? _____

5. What are the guide words on the page? _____ and _____

Bonus Box: On the back of this paper, write a sentence using each word.

How To Extend The Lesson:

- Use the reproducible for vocabulary development in all content areas. Have students look up words that relate to a science lesson, social-studies concept, or literature theme.

- Introduce a word of the week by writing it on the board and instructing students to find its definition. Give a copy of the award below to each student who uses the word correctly in a sentence during the week.

- Use the reproducible to reinforce word pairs. Give students one word of a pair to use for Word One on the paper, and have them complete the pair by using its synonym, antonym, or homophone for Word Two.

- Play a game to provide practice with guide words and parts of speech. Tell students to find a dictionary page labeled with a specific set of guide words. Then instruct students to look on that page to find an entry word for each category: noun, verb, and adjective. Call on volunteers to announce the entry word, naming its part of speech and definition. Continue playing until every student has volunteered an answer.

CONGRATULATIONS

to_____

for capturing the meaning of a new word.

Word:_____

Meaning:_____

Spin A Story Wheel

Reinforce literary elements with this spin-off of the traditional story map.

Skill: Mapping story elements

Estimated Lesson Time: 30 minutes

Teacher Preparation:
1. Duplicate page 55 for each student.
2. Select a story the class has read.

Materials:
1 copy of page 55 per student

Teacher Reference:

author: the person who wrote the book

character: a person appearing in the story

illustrator: the person who created the pictures in the book

plot: the structure of a story, including the problems or challenges that a character faces in the story line

setting: where the story takes place

title: the name of the book

Introducing The Lesson:

Tell students that they will be using information from the selected story to complete a story wheel. To get things rolling, have each student stand up and tell one thing about the story, such as a plot detail, a character, or an emotional response he had to the story.

Steps:

1. Provide time for students to discuss their reactions to the story.

2. Distribute page 55 to each student.

3. Challenge students to complete the Bonus Box activity.

Who was your favorite character?

Where did the story take place?

Which character was mentioned first?

Did the setting of the story change?

Who was the most important character?

What problem occurred?

How was the problem solved?

Which character are you most like?

Which character are you least like?

What was your favorite part of the story?

Name _____

Story Wheel

Complete the wheel with information from the story.
Then write a sentence about the story around the
outline of the wheel.

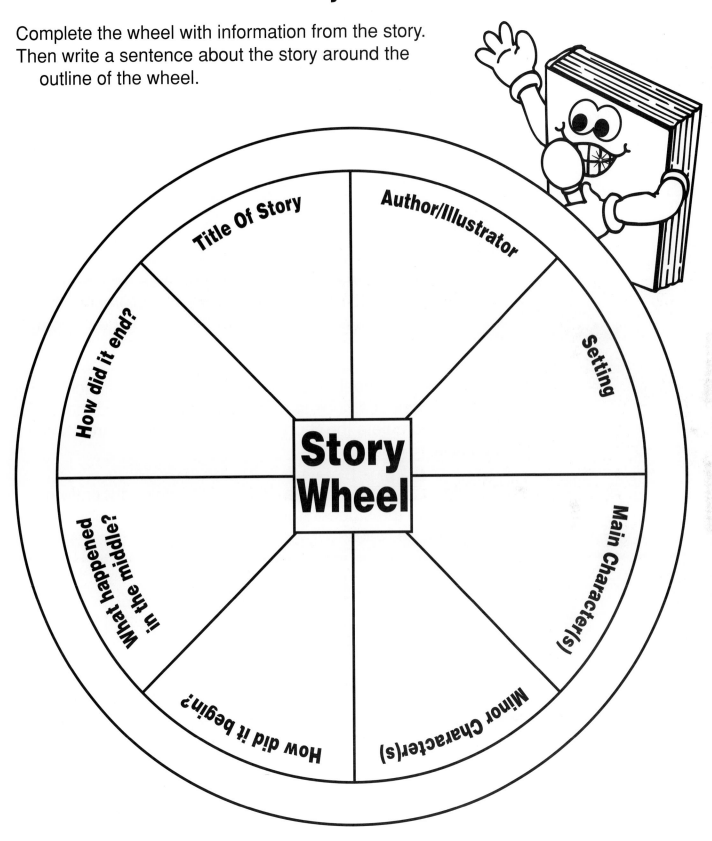

How To Extend The Lesson:

- Have each student select a character from the story. Ask her to imagine what it might be like to spend the day with that character. Instruct each student to write a paragraph telling about the imagined day.

- Let the setting of the book inspire an art activity. Have each student select a scene from the story to illustrate using watercolors or colored chalk.

- Use the Story Wheel for a cooperative-learning activity. Divide students into eight groups. Assign a section of the Story Wheel to each group. Have all the groups record their information on one enlarged copy of the wheel; then display the finished product.

- Use the Story Wheel as a book-report form. Allow each student to select a book to read. After she has read the book, have her complete the Story Wheel form, then share it with the class.

- Provide each student with a copy of the bookmark pattern below. Have the student track his reading progress by listing each book he reads.

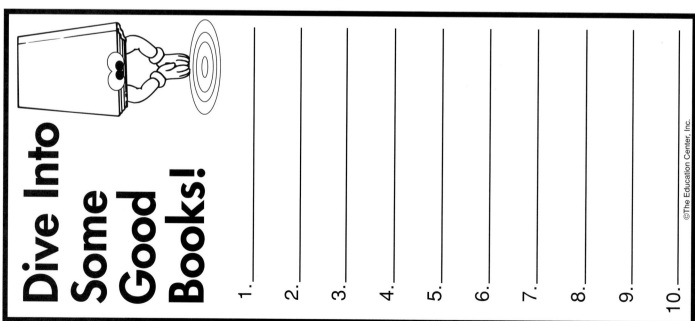

Dive Into Some Good Books!

1.
2.
3.
4.
5.
6.
7.
8.
9.
10.

©The Education Center, Inc.

Picture-Perfect Grammar

Nouns and verbs abound in this picture-related grammar search for these parts of speech.

Skill: Identifying nouns and verbs

Estimated Lesson Time: 30 minutes

Teacher Preparation:
1. Duplicate page 59 for each student.
2. Gather the materials listed below.

Materials:
1 copy of page 59 per student
crayons (optional)

Teacher Reference:
Common nouns indicate a class of persons, places, and things. (girl, city, car)
Pronouns take the place of nouns. (I, you, he)
Proper nouns name a particular person, place, or thing. (Andy, Arizona, Coke®)
Verbs are words that show action, state of being, or occurance.
Linking verbs are followed by a word or phrase that modifies the subject of a sentence. (Randy *is* tall.)

Introducing The Lesson:

Ask each student to look around the room and inconspicuously observe one of his classmates. Instruct the student to notice five things about the classmate. After a given time, ask students to volunteer their observations while you list them on the board. When the responses have been recorded, ask students to categorize them into naming words and action words.

Steps:

1. Reinforce for students the fact that naming words are called *nouns* and that action words are called *verbs*.

2. Distribute a copy of page 59 to each student.

3. Provide time for students to observe the picture and create lists of nouns and verbs. If time allows, have students color the picture.

4. Challenge students to complete the Bonus Box activity.

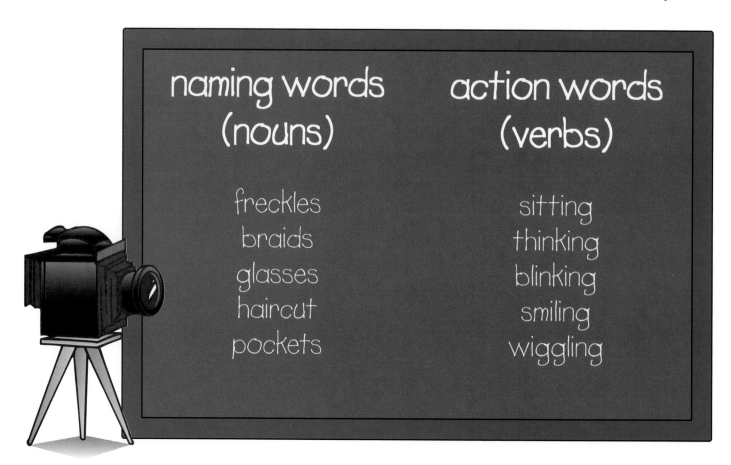

naming words
(nouns)

freckles
braids
glasses
haircut
pockets

action words
(verbs)

sitting
thinking
blinking
smiling
wiggling

Picture-Perfect Grammar

Look at the picture.
List examples of nouns and verbs shown in the picture.

Nouns		Verbs	
_____	_____	_____	_____
_____	_____	_____	_____
_____	_____	_____	_____
_____	_____	_____	_____
_____	_____	_____	_____

Bonus Box: On the back of the paper, list five nouns and verbs that are *not* in the picture.

How To Extend The Lesson:

- If weather permits, take students outdoors to observe children on your school playground. Challenge them to find a predetermined amount of nouns and verbs as they observe the playground scene.

- Place students in small groups. Distribute a copy of the same picture to each group. (If desired, use the example shown below.) Have each group try to find as many examples of nouns and verbs as possible in the picture, and then record them in a list. After a certain amount of time, ask for a total number from each group; then check the word lists together.

- Have students look through old magazines for pictures that contain examples of nouns and verbs. Have them work individually or with partners to create lists for their pictures.

- Reverse the lesson by giving the students a list of nouns and verbs and then having them create pictures showing examples of the words. Provide time for students to show their pictures to the class.

- Have students brainstorm nouns and verbs associated with the current holiday or season. Give each student a sheet of drawing paper to illustrate and label the nouns and verbs.

Absolutely Adjectives

Lead your students on a mission for description, and watch some awesome adjectives appear!

Skill: Using adjectives

Estimated Lesson Time: 30 minutes

Teacher Preparation:
1. Duplicate page 63 for each student.
2. Gather the materials listed below.

Materials:
1 copy of page 63 per student
1 self-stick note per student

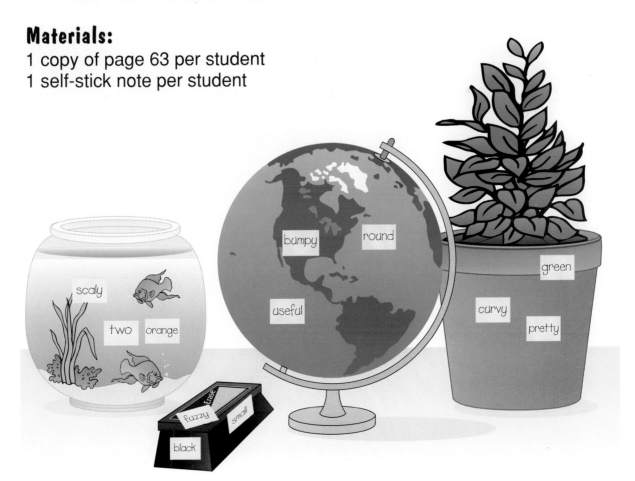

Introducing The Lesson:

Tell students to look around the room and notice signs of description. Remind students that description words, or adjectives, can tell about size, shape, color, number, or a certain quality of an object. After students have observed the classroom for several minutes, distribute a self-stick note to each student. Instruct the student to pick out an object and write a describing word for it on the note. Then have each student attach her note to the object it describes.

Steps:

1. After students return to their desks, walk around the room and read the notes aloud.

2. Ask students to identify each adjective as one describing size, shape, color, number, or a certain quality.

3. Tell students that they are going to continue making observations about descriptions as they complete the information on the reproducible.

4. Challenge students to complete the Bonus Box activity.

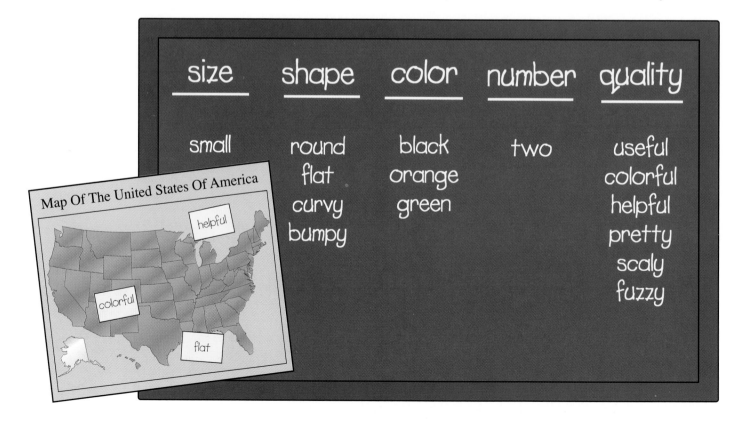

Absolutely Adjectives

List ten objects that you see in the room.
Then write adjectives that describe each object.

Objects   **Description Words**

1. _____   _____

2. _____   _____

3. _____   _____

4. _____   _____

5. _____   _____

6. _____   _____

7. _____   _____

8. _____   _____

9. _____   _____

10. _____   _____

Choose three of the objects on your list.
Write a descriptive sentence about each object.

1. _____

2. _____

3. _____

Bonus Box: On the back of the paper, list the senses you used in describing the objects.

How To Extend The Lesson:

- Have students compare the objects they described. List the adjectives used for a common object. As a class, compose a paragraph using all the descriptions students listed for that object.

- Have students use the information on their reproducibles for a descriptive writing assignment. Then supply each student with a piece of drawing paper to illustrate his description.

- Incorporate art appreciation into a reinforcement activity by displaying a copy of a famous work of art and having each student list ten adjectives to describe it. Discuss the words on the lists to explore students' reactions to the art.

- Place students in cooperative groups and challenge each group to list as many adjectives as possible to describe a topic, such as ice cream or feathers. Compare the lists as a review of descriptive word choices.

- Introduce an adjective a day by writing an unusual or unfamiliar adjective on the board. Have students find the word in the dictionary. Challenge the students to use the word at least twice during the day.

droll	savory	elaborate
corpulent	sluggish	humdrum
loquacious	mischievous	beneficial
blissful	tranquil	jubilant
tedious	skittish	sullen
petite	hideous	irascible
ample	wretched	peevish
perilous	outlandish	enthralling

Sentence Shenanigans

Tickle your students' funny bones with this light-hearted look at sentence structure.

Skill: Identifying subjects and predicates

Estimated Lesson Time: 45 minutes

Teacher Preparation:
1. Duplicate page 67 for each student.
2. Obtain an example of items commonly paired together (see materials).

Materials:
1 copy of page 67 per student
an example of items commonly paired together, such as peanut butter and jelly, macaroni and cheese, or a hammer and nail

Background Information:
• A subject consists of the main noun (or a group of words acting as the main noun) and tells what the sentence is about.

• A predicate contains a verb and sometimes a group of words related to the verb. It describes something about the subject.

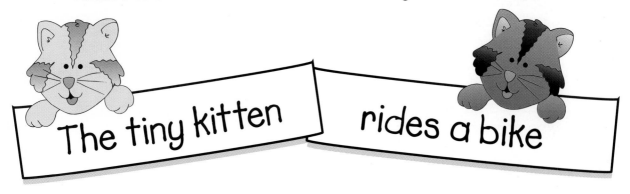

The tiny kitten   rides a bike

Introducing The Lesson:

Show students an example of items that are commonly paired together. Ask students to name some other items that create pairs. List their responses on the board. Remind students that a sentence is made up of a very important pair: a *subject* and a *predicate.* Review the definitions of subject and predicate with your students. Tell the class that they will be pairing together an assortment of subjects and predicates to come up with some interesting and unusual sentences.

Steps:

1. Distribute a copy of page 67 to each student.

2. Instruct students to compose subjects and predicates in the appropriate sections of the reproducible, then cut apart the completed sections.

3. Gather the sections and place in two stacks, one for subjects and one for predicates.

4. Ask a student volunteer to draw a section from each stack, then write the two sections on the board as a complete sentence. Direct the student to read the sentence to the class, then identify the subject and the predicate in the sentence.

5. Continue the activity until each student has had a turn, or as time allows.

6. Challenge students to complete the Bonus Box activity.

The big dog | wagged his tail

subject   predicate

Sentence Shenanigans

Write the subject of a sentence in each box and then cut the boxes apart. Example:

The tiny kitten

Subject
Subject
Subject

Write the predicate of a sentence in each box and then cut the boxes apart. Example:

rides a bike

Predicate
Predicate
Predicate

Follow your teacher's directions to make sentences with the subjects and predicates.

Bonus Box: Draw a picture to illustrate one of the completed sentences.

How To Extend The Lesson:

- Have students work in pairs to compose a list of ten subjects and a list of ten predicates. Have each student pair trade its subject list with another pair of students. Instruct each pair to use the new subject list and the predicate list to create ten sentences. Provide time for each pair to read a few of the sentences to the class.

- Select a student each day to be the Official Daily Subject. Have the class use the student's name as the subject in sentence-writing practice.

- Ask students to brainstorm a list of predicates that describe things the students do in the course of a school day. Have each student write one of the predicates on a sentence strip. Post the completed strips on a bulletin board with the subject "Third-Grade Students…"

- Divide the class into two teams for a game of subject-and-predicate baseball. The team who is "at bat" stands in a line while the other team's members stay at their desks to await their turn at bat. "Pitch" a sentence to the first player in line. The student listens to the sentence, then must identify the subject (or predicate) of the sentence. If he is correct, he walks to a desk designated as first base. (Also designate a second base, third base, and home plate.) If he is incorrect, he sits down at his desk to indicate an "out." Play continues as the next player in line repeats the routine. Award a point for each player that makes it back to home plate. Call the second team to bat when the first team has earned three outs.

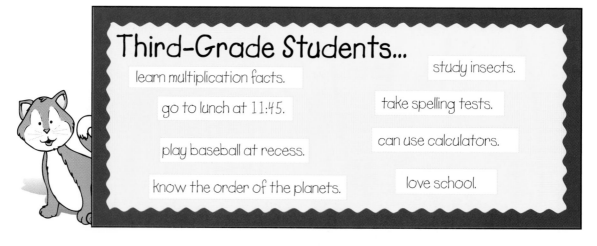

Third-Grade Students…

learn multiplication facts.

go to lunch at 11:45.

play baseball at recess.

know the order of the planets.

study insects.

take spelling tests.

can use calculators.

love school.

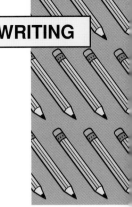

It's In The Bag!

Encourage creative thinking with this story starter that provides an unlimited flow of ideas.

 Skill: Practicing creative writing

 Estimated Lesson Time: 45 minutes

Teacher Preparation:

1. Duplicate page 71 for each student.
2. Place three or four small, varied objects in a paper bag. (The objects can be an assortment of unrelated items, such as a gum wrapper, a comb, a magnifying glass, and a marble.)

Materials:

1 copy of page 71 per student
1 paper bag containing several small objects

Introducing The Lesson:

Tell students that you have a bag with a big story in it. Explain that the bag contains several objects that relate to the story. Take the objects from the bag one by one, allowing the class to observe and comment on each item.

Steps:

1. After students have observed the contents of the bag, distribute a copy of page 71 to each student and tell him to write a story that includes the objects in the story line.

2. Challenge students to complete the Bonus Box activity.

Who are the characters?

Where does the story take place?

How is each object important to the story?

It's In The Bag!

List the objects in the bag. Then write a story about the objects.

Objects: _____   _____   _____   _____

Bonus Box: Give your story a title. Then draw a picture of one of the objects from the story.

How To Extend The Lesson:

• Provide time for students to share their stories from page 71 with the class. Then have students categorize their stories into genres such as mystery, humor, fantasy, realistic fiction, and science fiction.

• Have students illustrate their stories by drawing with crayon on paper lunch sacks. Display the pictures and stories on a bulletin board titled "The Story Is In The Bag."

• Ask for student volunteers to bring bags of objects from home. Place the bags in a center and let students choose one to write about.

• After reading a story as a class, have students create a bag of items that relate to the story. Send an empty bag home with each student to fill with several items that are significant to the story.

Lunar Letters

Neither rain nor sleet nor dark of night will stop your students from learning letter-writing skills!

Skill: Writing a friendly letter

Estimated Lesson Time: 30 minutes

Teacher Preparation:

1. Duplicate page 75 for each student.
2. Write the model of a friendly letter from page 74 on the board.

Materials:

1 copy of page 75 per student

Background Information:

The parts of a friendly letter are:

- *heading:* includes the sender's address and the date the letter was written
- *greeting:* tells to whom the letter was written
- *body:* tells what the letter is about
- *closing:* brings the letter to a close
- *signature:* tells who wrote the letter

Introducing The Lesson:

Tell your students to imagine that they have the opportunity to go on an amazing field trip to the moon! The only catch is that they have to leave shortly, and will not have time to talk to their parents before they go. Have each student write a letter to her parents explaining the situation.

Steps:

1. Write the sample letter below on the board showing students the five parts of a friendly letter.

2. Distribute a copy of page 75 to each student.

3. Challenge students to complete the Bonus Box activity.

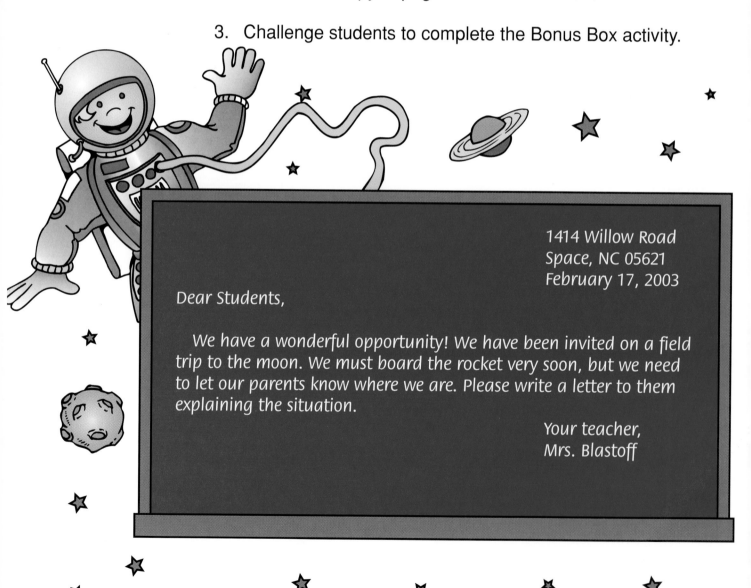

1414 Willow Road
Space, NC 05621
February 17, 2003

Dear Students,

  We have a wonderful opportunity! We have been invited on a field trip to the moon. We must board the rocket very soon, but we need to let our parents know where we are. Please write a letter to them explaining the situation.

Your teacher,
Mrs. Blastoff

Name ____________________

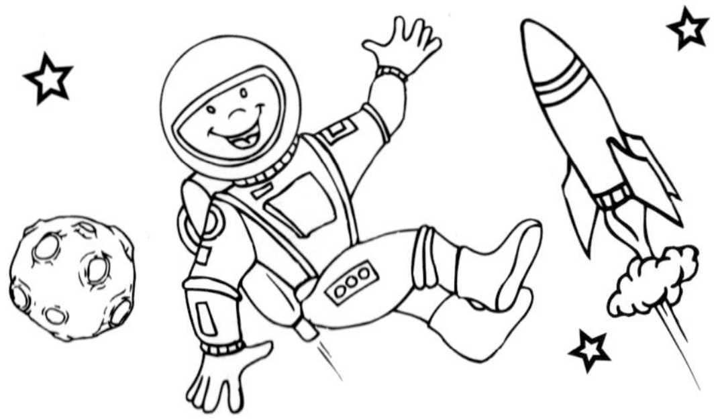

☆ Lunar Letters

Bonus Box: On the back of the paper, design a stamp to illustrate the contents of your letter.

How To Extend This Lesson:

- Have each student write another letter to show how he thinks his parents would respond to the field-trip letter.

- Have each student write a letter telling about his field trip to the moon.

- Find a company for the children to write to asking for a pamphlet, a sample, or some other information. Show the children how to correctly address an envelope with their return addresses and the company's address.

- If possible, arrange a field trip to a post office. Let students see how the mail is sorted for delivery.

- Ask students to bring postmarked envelopes from mail they have received at home. Place the envelopes in a center with a large map. Have students use the map to locate the origins of each postmark.

- Share a story that focuses on letter writing. *The Jolly Postman: Or Other People's Letters* by Janet and Allan Ahlberg (Little, Brown and Company; 1986) follows a postman through the land of fairy tales, and lets you peek inside some very interesting envelopes!

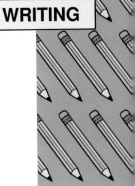

Paragraph-Writing Recipe

When students follow this basic recipe for paragraph writing, they will get gourmet results!

Skill: Writing a paragraph

Estimated Lesson Time: 30 minutes

Teacher Preparation:

1. Duplicate page 79 for each student.
2. Provide a class supply of cookies.

Materials:

1 copy of page 79 per student
1 cookie per student

Cook up a paragraph
with these tasty topics:
• your favorite sport
• a famous person
• a hobby
• a science concept
• social studies information
• a holiday
• a book or movie character

Introducing The Lesson:

Begin your lesson by distributing a cookie to each student. Tell students to take a bite; then have them list some of the ingredients typically found in cookies. After naming possible ingredients, discuss the steps that are followed when baking cookies.

Steps:

1. Tell students that they will follow a recipe to "cook up" a paragraph. They will have to gather the necessary ingredients, then follow the steps for putting the paragraph together.

2. Distribute a copy of page 79 to each student.

3. Challenge students to complete the Bonus Box activity.

sugar

butter

flour

vanilla

chocolate chips

1. Preheat the oven.
2. Mix the ingredients.
3. Drop spoonfuls onto a cookie sheet.
4. Bake in the oven.
5. Cool on a wire rack.

Recipe For A Red-Hot Paragraph

Gather the ingredients listed below.
Then follow the steps to complete the paragraph.

Ingredients:

• one topic:_____

• explain how you know about the topic: _____

_____

• two facts about the topic:

_____

_____

• an opinion about the topic:

_____

Steps:

1. Begin with a sentence announcing the topic. Write it below.
2. Follow with a sentence explaining how you know about the topic.
3. Take one fact and write a sentence with it.
4. Add another sentence with the second fact.
5. Supply an opinion about the topic for a finishing touch.

_____

_____

_____

_____

_____

_____

_____

Bonus Box: Proofread your paragraph. Underline your topic sentence with a blue crayon. Highlight each capital letter with a yellow crayon. Highlight each punctuation mark with a red crayon.

How To Extend The Lesson:

- Have each student read his paragraph from page 79 to the class. After each student reads, have him state the main idea of the paragraph.

- Use the recipe format as a science or social studies review. Assign a topic from either subject for students to explain in paragraph form.

- Incorporate show-and-tell with paragraph writing. Ask each student to write a paragraph about the object he would like to present. Have him read his paragraph to tell about the object he shows to the class.

- Have students write a paragraph as a cooperative group activity. Place students in groups of five. Tell each student in the group to write one of the sentences for the paragraph. Have each group present its completed paragraph to the class.

- Write each sentence of a paragraph on a separate sentence strip. Have students place the strips in logical order to form a paragraph.

- Have students prepare a batch of No-Bake Nibbles. After each student samples the treat, instruct her to write a paragraph about her favorite snack.

No-Bake Nibbles

You will need:
1 cup honey
1 1/2 cups powdered milk
1 1/2 cups wheat germ
1/2 cup raisins
1/2 cup chocolate chips
Combine all ingredients together.
Shape into small balls.
Eat and enjoy!

Looking Into The Future

Travel on a futuristic journey as penned through your students' descriptive writing.

Skill: Practicing descriptive writing

Estimated Lesson Time: 45 minutes

Teacher Preparation:
1. Duplicate page 83 for each student.
2. Gather the materials listed below.

Materials:
1 copy of page 83 per student
1 sheet of 6 3/4" x 9" blank paper per student

Introducing The Lesson:

Tell students that their writing assignment involves a time travel adventure to the past and then to the future. Ask students to imagine what their lives would have been like 100 years ago. Tell them to think about styles in clothing, methods of transportation, forms of entertainment, and types of occupations from the past and compare them to what we have today. Record students' responses on the board. Next tell students to use their imaginations to predict what the future will bring for each of those categories. Explain that they will use their predictions to create a futuristic magazine.

Steps:

1. Provide each student with a copy of page 83 and one sheet of blank paper.

2. Instruct the student to cut out the cover and fold it on the thin line. Then fold the blank page in half.

3. Have students insert the folded blank page into the cover and staple them together on the left-hand side to form the magazine.

4. Tell students to fill in the blanks for the date and name, then label each blank page with one of the following titles: Clothing, Transportation, Entertainment, and Occupations.

5. Instruct students to illustrate each page with items from the future, then write a descriptive paragraph under each illustration.

6. Have each student complete the information on the back cover.

7. Provide time for students to share their completed magazines with the class.

Looking Into The Future

Predicts Life

_____
(name)

In The Year

_____
(date)

Self-Portrait

About The Author

The author was born on _____

As a child the author enjoyed _____

_____

The author's wish for the future is _____

_____

Bonus Box: Decorate and color magazine cover.

How To Extend The Lesson:

- Encourage students to add pages to their magazines describing other topics for the future.

- Invite students to create and wear their own future fashions. Then host a fashion show of the future.

- Instruct each student to write about something he hopes will not be changed in the future. Ask volunteers to share their papers with the class.

- Create a bulletin board using cutouts of students' handprints traced on colored construction paper. Have each student trace his hand, cut out the resulting shape, and write a sentence on the shape describing a hope he has for the future. Arrange the cutouts on the bulletin board and add the title "The Future Is In Our Hands."

I hope one day I'll be used to discover far-off planets.

THE FUTURE IS IN OUR HANDS

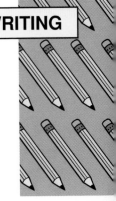

Ready, Set, Edit!

Capitalize on this unusual story starter to promote students' editing skills.

Skill: Editing

Estimated Lesson Time: 40 minutes

Teacher Preparation:
Duplicate page 87 for each student.

Materials:
1 copy of page 87 per student

Topic List

holidays
animals
recycling
favorite books
types of music
plants
desserts
games
school subjects
types of shoes

Introducing The Lesson:

Ask students to stand up and turn their desks around so that they are facing the opposite direction. Have students sit down in this new arrangement. Ask for their reactions to the new arrangement. Then have students imagine what it would be like if their school day happened in the opposite order. Ask for several ideas; then tell students to use those ideas (as well as any others they may have) to complete a writing and editing assignment.

Steps:

1. Distribute a copy of page 87 to each student.

2. Ask each student to write down on the reproducible the topic of the assignment and three ideas relating to the topic.

3. Have students refer to their three ideas as they write a story on a separate sheet of paper.

4. Instruct students to edit their completed work using the form on the reproducible.

5. Have students make any necessary corrections.

6. Challenge students to complete the Bonus Box activity.

Topic: Sports
1. baseball
2. football
3. basketball

Topic: Fishing
1. bait
2. lures
3. casting

Topic: Pets
1. cats
2. dogs
3. hamsters

Name _____ *Editing*

Ready, Set, Edit!

Use this outline to help you think of ideas for your writing.
Then edit your work with the form below.

My topic: _____

Idea for paragraph one: _____

_____

Idea for paragraph two: _____

_____

Idea for paragraph three: _____

_____

Editing My Work	Yes	No
I used each one of the ideas in a paragraph.		
I indented the first word of each paragraph.		
I used the correct punctuation at the end of each sentence.		
I used a capital letter at the beginning of each sentence.		
I checked for spelling mistakes.		
I used neat handwriting.		

Bonus Box: Trade papers with a friend. Proofread each other's work.

How To Extend The Lesson:

- Provide a teacher-created writing sample that contains several errors. Have students use the checklist on page 87 to help spot the errors, then rewrite the sample correctly.

- Show students some basic proofreading marks as shown on the chart below. Practice using the marks with a writing sample copied onto an overhead transparency. Have student volunteers show how to use the marks as the class edits the writing sample together.

- Use the reproducible on page 87 with other writing topics. If desired, use the activity once a week to reinforce proofreading and editing skills.

- Keep and date several writing samples for each student in individual portfolios. Each grading period, have students look over their writing samples and evaluate their progress.

Proofreading Marks

Instruction	Mark In Text	Mark In Text	Corrected Text
delete	ℯ	the ~~bad~~ dog	the dog
make capital	cap	the dog	The dog
make lowercase	lc	the Dog	the dog
spell out	sp	②dogs	two dogs
insert comma	∧	dogs dogs dogs	dogs, dogs, dogs
insert period	⊙	See the dogs⊙	See the dogs.
start paragraph	¶	"Do you see the dog?"¶"I don't see it."	"Do you see the dog?" "I don't see it."

Math Fact Attack

Your students will be abuzz as they practice basic math operations.

Skill: Reviewing addition and subtraction

Estimated Lesson Time: 30 minutes

Teacher Preparation:
Duplicate page 91 for each student.

Materials:
1 copy of page 91 per student

Teacher Reference:
Students can generate math problems by counting these classroom objects:

- chalkboard erasers
- student chairs
- teacher chairs
- tables
- desks
- computers
- bulletin boards
- light fixtures
- musical instruments
- lunchboxes

Introducing The Lesson:

Tell students that you became so involved in the book you were reading that you lost track of time and were unable to prepare the math lesson for the day. You know how disappointed the students are, so you will enlist their help in creating a math lesson with information they find in the classroom.

Steps:

1. Ask all students with summer birthdays to stand up. Then ask all students with winter birthdays to raise their hands. Record the number of students in each group on the board, and ask for a volunteer to create a math problem using the information (the numbers of students in both groups could be added together for a total or subtracted to find the difference).

2. Distribute a copy of page 91 to each student. Read the information with your students. Repeat the procedure for finding the information necessary to create the math problems. Then have students solve the problems independently.

3. Challenge students to complete the Bonus Box activity.

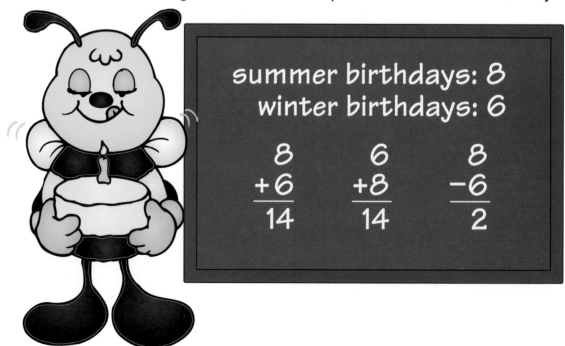

summer birthdays: 8
winter birthdays: 6

$$\begin{array}{r} 8 \\ +6 \\ \hline 14 \end{array} \qquad \begin{array}{r} 6 \\ +8 \\ \hline 14 \end{array} \qquad \begin{array}{r} 8 \\ -6 \\ \hline 2 \end{array}$$

Math Fact Attack

Find the information needed to create each math problem.
Write the problem in the box.
Then answer each problem.

1. The number of students with blue eyes plus the number of students with brown eyes.

    1.

2. The number of buttons worn by the oldest student plus the number of buttons worn by the youngest student.

    2.

3. The number of students who brought their lunch plus the number of students who bought their lunch from the cafeteria.

    3.

4. The number of students wearing pants minus the number of students wearing dresses.

    4.

5. The number of students in the room minus the number of boys in the room.

    5.

6. The number of students in the room minus the number of girls in the room.

    6.

7. The number of flags in the room plus the number of fingers the teacher is holding up.

    7.

8. The number of doors in the room plus your age.

    8.

9. The number of trash cans in the room minus the number of pencil sharpeners.

    9.

10. The number of problems on this paper minus the number of teachers in the room.

    10.

Bonus Box: Write a math problem on the back of this paper. Use information about the classroom in the problem.

How To Extend The Lesson:

- Have students check their answers on the reproducible by demonstrating the information in each problem. Have students stand up to represent the numbers requested in the student-related problems. Have them draw diagrams to show problems that require objects in the room.

- Have students take a survey of another classroom and class to find the information requested on the reproducible. Have them complete the reproducible again with the new information.

- Ask students to try using a different operation to solve each problem on the reproducible. Discuss which problems can be worked and which ones can't be done.

- Distribute a copy of the pattern below to each student. Instruct the student to assemble the pattern to form a number cube. Place students in pairs. Each student rolls her number cube. The pair creates as many math problems as possible using the numbers they have rolled.

Regrouping Rally

*Help students reach the winner's circle as they use
regrouping to find the sums.*

Skill: Regrouping with 2-digit addition

Estimated Lesson Time: 45 minutes

Teacher Preparation:
1. Duplicate the reproducible on page 95 for each student.
2. Gather the supplies listed below.

Materials:
1 copy of page 95 per student
classroom set of Cuisenaire® Rods (or use the patterns provided
on page 313)
1 die for each pair of students
1 blue and 1 red crayon per student

Quick Tip:
Help your students create straight columns while working on math problems
with this easy tip. Instruct students to turn a sheet of lined notebook paper
sideways and use the lines as column dividers. The lines help students keep
each numeral in its correct place!

Introducing The Lesson:

Ask your students if they have seen or heard of a rally. Explain that a rally is a long-distance car race. Tell students that as a warm-up for a regrouping rally, they will play a game to practice regrouping ones into tens. Remind students that when they add numbers in a column, the numbers must be regrouped to the next place value when the sum reaches ten or more.

Steps:

1. Place students in pairs. Give each pair 20 unit cubes, 20 tens rods, 1 hundreds square, and 1 die.

2. Have each partner take turns rolling the die. The student counts out the number of unit cubes indicated on the die. When he gets ten or more cubes, he must trade for a tens rod. The first player to trade tens rods for a hundreds square is the winner.

3. After several rounds of play, distribute a copy of page 95 to each student.

4. Allow time for each student to complete the reproducible. Then challenge students to complete the Bonus Box activity.

I have 13 cubes. I can trade in 10 of the cubes for a tens rod.

Regrouping Rally

Add to find the sums.
You will have to regroup to solve some of the problems.

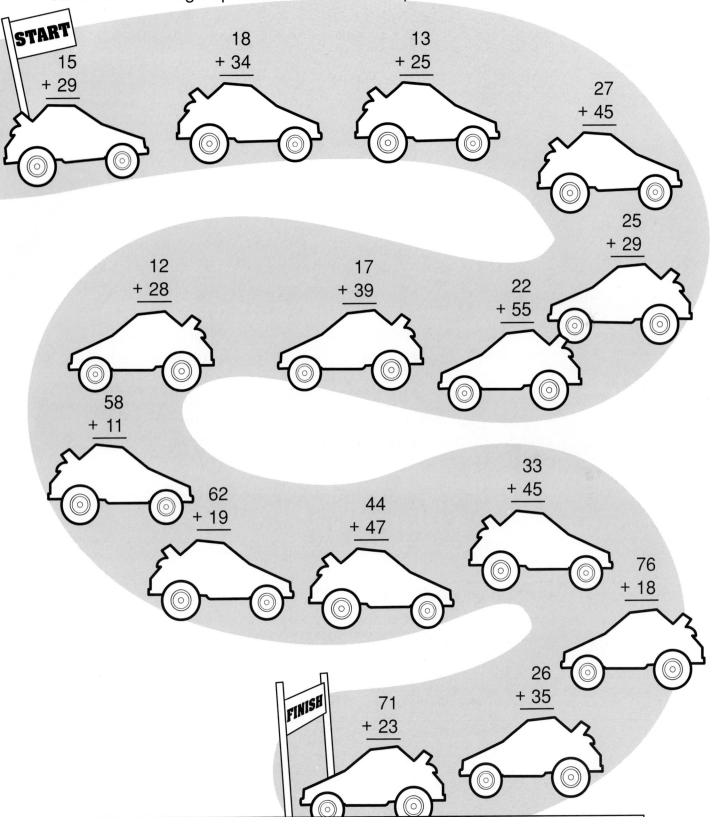

START

15
+ 29

18
+ 34

13
+ 25

27
+ 45

25
+ 29

12
+ 28

17
+ 39

22
+ 55

58
+ 11

62
+ 19

44
+ 47

33
+ 45

76
+ 18

26
+ 35

FINISH

71
+ 23

Bonus Box: If you had to regroup, color the car's wheels red. If you did not regroup, color the car's wheels blue.

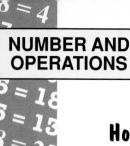

How To Extend The Lesson:

- Ask each student to create one addition problem that requires re-grouping and one that does not need regrouping. Collect the problems and write them on an overhead transparency. Have the students try to identify which problems will need to be regrouped before they actually solve the problems.

- Prepare an easy-to-update center activity that will reinforce regrouping practice. Program a strip of tagboard with a list of ten numbers; then laminate for durability. Post the list in a center. Use a wipe-off marker to write an operation (such as +14) at the top of the list. Instruct each student to copy the ten math problems on a sheet of paper and solve them. The next day, wipe off the old operation and replace it with a new one. The center will have ten new problems to solve!

- Practice regrouping with an activity that will keep students on the move. Have each student write a two-digit number on a self-stick note and attach it to her shirt. Instruct each student to carry a pencil and pa-per with her as you place the students in two lines, facing each other. At your signal, the two students facing each other write and solve an addition problem using the numbers on their self-stick notes. Then have the students in each line rotate one position. Repeat the proce-dure until a desired number of problems have been solved.

- Have each student create a word problem that will require regrouping to solve. Ask for student volunteers to write their problems on the board for their classmates to solve. For an added challenge, have students include unnecessary information in their word problems.

Sally had 39 pennies. Her sister gave her 42 more pennies and 15 nickels. How many pennies does Sally have now?

Jerry has 14 rabbits and 16 birds. He feeds his pets twice a day. How many pets does he own?

Subtraction Snack Shack

*Send your little piggies to market for a shopping spree
that reinforces the concept of regrouping.*

Skill: Regrouping with 2-digit subtraction

Estimated Lesson Time: 45 minutes

Teacher Preparation:

1. Duplicate page 99 for each student.
2. Gather the materials listed below.
3. Write "90¢" on the chalkboard.

Materials:

1 copy of page 99 per student

class set of index cards, each programmed with a coin value ranging from 5¢ to 29¢ (The number in the ones place of each number should be 5 or larger.)

Teacher Reference:

Use the term *regrouping* with your students instead of "borrowing" or "trading." The term *regrouping* is used in both addition and subtraction, and the student will have a better understanding of the concept if the same term is used when discussing either operation.

Introducing The Lesson:

Tell students that they are going to participate in a little spending spree. Write the amount "90¢" on the chalkboard, and distribute to each student an index card programmed with a coin value. Have each student in turn come to the board and subtract the amount written on his card from the total value. When the total reaches 0, or if it becomes too low to subtract from, begin again with 90¢ and continue until each student has had a turn.

Steps:

1. As each student subtracts his coin amount, discuss the rules for regrouping.

2. After each student has had a turn, distribute a copy of page 99 to each student.

3. Provide time for students to complete the reproducible.

4. Challenge students to complete the Bonus Box activity.

Subtraction Snack Shack

Use the picture to help solve each problem.
Show your work in each box.

THE SNACK SHACK

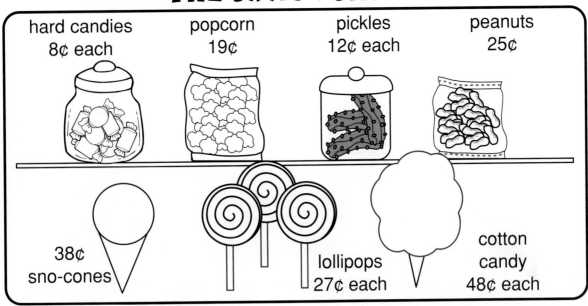

hard candies
8¢ each

popcorn
19¢

pickles
12¢ each

peanuts
25¢

38¢
sno-cones

lollipops
27¢ each

cotton
candy
48¢ each

Joe's Snack Attack

Joe has 90¢.
He bought a sno-cone.
How much money is left?

Then Joe bought some peanuts.
How much money is left?

Joe also bought popcorn.
How much money is left?

What could Joe buy with the money left over?

_____

Jane's Snack Attack

Jane has 90¢.
She bought cotton candy.
How much money is left?

Then Jane bought a lollipop.
How much money is left?

Jane also bought a pickle.
How much money is left?

What could Jane buy with the money left over?

_____

Bonus Box: What would you buy from the Snack Shack with 90¢? Make a list on the back of this paper.

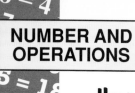

How To Extend The Lesson:

- Bring a jar of pennies to class. Instruct each student to take two pennies from the jar and write down the date from each penny. Have the student subtract the last two digits of the older date from the last two digits of the newer date (unless the newer date is 2000 or later). Then have the student return the pennies to the jar and repeat the procedure until he has created ten problems.

- Play a version of Hangman using subtraction problems. Write a subtraction problem that requires regrouping on the board. Ask a student volunteer to come to the board to solve the problem. If the student solves the problem correctly, write a tally mark on the board. If the student answers incorrectly, draw a part of the hangman on the board. Challenge the class to earn ten tally marks before you complete the hangman drawing.

- Distribute a supply of plastic coins (or use the coin patterns on page 314) so that each student has an amount less than $1.00. Place each student with a partner and have the pair determine the value of each partner's coins. Then instruct each pair to write and solve a subtraction problem using the two coin amounts. Have students switch partners and repeat the process until a determined number of problems have been written and solved.

- Duplicate a supply of the patterns below to create subtraction problems for a math center activity. Program the patterns with subtraction problems that require regrouping, as well as with problems where regrouping is not required. Program the back of each pattern for self-checking.

©The Education Center, Inc. • *Ready-to-Go Lessons* • TEC1116

Scrambled Numbers

Reinforce place value and number sense with this "egg-citing" lesson!

Skill: Determining place value to the thousands

Estimated Lesson Time: 30 minutes

Teacher Preparation:
1. Duplicate a copy of page 103 for each student.
2. Program an index card with a numeral from 0 to 9 for each student.

Materials:
1 copy of page 103 per student
1 programmed index card per student

Teacher Reference:
Reinforce the concept of place value by having students determine if the following items would number in the ones, tens, hundreds, or thousands:

- names in the phone book
- toothpicks in a box
- pieces of popcorn in a bowl
- students in a classroom
- items on a fast-food menu
- different types of cookies in the grocery store
- hairs on a person's head
- bananas in a bunch
- keys on a computer
- pieces of bubble gum in a pack
- books in the library
- letters in a first name
- fish in an aquarium

Introducing The Lesson:

Tell students that they are going to work together to scramble numbers into different place values. Distribute a programmed index card to each student. Inform each student that the numeral on her card may take on the value of ones, tens, hundreds, or thousands.

Steps:

1. Call four students to come to the front of the room with their index cards. Instruct them to hold their cards in front of them so that the class can observe each numeral.

2. Ask a student volunteer to arrange the students so that their numerals make the largest (or smallest) possible number.

3. Ask another volunteer to rearrange the students so that the largest (or smallest) numeral is in the hundreds (or tens) place.

4. Continue calling groups of four to the front of the room and asking volunteers to arrange them in designated numbers until all students have had a chance to participate.

5. Distribute a copy of page 103 to each student. Provide time for students to complete the reproducible.

6. Challenge students to complete the Bonus Box activity.

Scrambled Numbers

Follow the directions to create numbers for each group of numerals.

4, 3, 6, 2

Write the largest number. _____

Write the smallest number. _____

Write a number with the smallest numeral in the tens place. _____

Write a number with the largest numeral in the hundreds place. _____

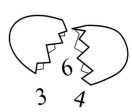

2, 9, 0, 6

Write the largest number. _____

Write the smallest number. _____

Write a number with the smallest numeral in the tens place. _____

Write a number with the largest numeral in the hundreds place. _____

7, 8, 1, 5

Write the largest number. _____

Write the smallest number. _____

Write a number with the smallest numeral in the tens place. _____

Write a number with the largest numeral in the hundreds place. _____

3, 0, 8, 4

Write the largest number. _____

Write the smallest number. _____

Write a number with the smallest numeral in the tens place. _____

Write a number with the largest numeral in the hundreds place. _____

2, 5, 1, 7

Write the largest number. _____

Write the smallest number. _____

Write a number with the smallest numeral in the tens place. _____

Write a number with the largest numeral in the hundreds place. _____

Bonus Box: Arrange the numbers you created with each set in order from least to greatest.

How To Extend The Lesson:

- Place students in groups of four. Give each group a die (or use copies of the die pattern on page 92). Instruct each student to roll the die four times and record the first roll as a numeral in the ones place, the second roll as a numeral in the tens place, the third roll as a numeral in the hundreds place, and the fourth roll as a numeral in the thousands place. After each group member has had a turn, have each member compare to see who rolled the highest number.

- Instruct each student to think of a four-digit number. Have the student use place-value blocks (or copies of the place-value patterns on page 313) to create a model of the number he selected. Then have the class arrange the models in order from least to greatest.

- Challenge students to collect 1,000 objects. Decide on an easy-to-count item to collect, such as soft-drink caps, pennies, or milk-jug lids. Designate a box in your room as the collection site. Provide time each week for a student to count the items in the box and place them in groups of ten. Secure each group of ten in a sandwich-size resealable bag. When ten sandwich-size bags have been filled, place them in a gallon-size bag. When ten gallon-size bags have been filled, your students have reached their goal!

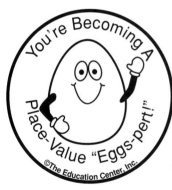

- Have each student write down the last four digits of his phone number. Have students work in small groups to determine who has the largest numeral in each position. Then have the group members determine who has the largest and the smallest four-digit number.

- Reward students for their hard work in determining place value with copies of the award tokens.

Number Roundup

Reinforce the concept of rounding numbers with this rootin'-tootin' activity.

Skill: Rounding numbers to the thousands place

Estimated Lesson Time: 30 minutes

Teacher Preparation:
1. Duplicate a copy of page 107 for each student.
2. Program a set of 20 index cards with numbers to be used for rounding. (See the examples on page 106.)

Materials:
1 copy of page 107 per student
a set of programmed index cards
20 index cards per student pair

Teacher Reference:
Remind students how to round numbers with these three steps:

Step 1: Find the place value of the numeral to be rounded.　　**4,902**

Step 2: Look at the digit to its right.　　**4,902**
↑
If the digit is less than five, round the numeral down.
If the digit is five or greater, round the numeral up.

Step 3: Change each digit to the right of the rounded numeral to zero.
5,000

7,350

1,099

9,502

3,499

2,813

6,423

5,912

6,794

4,533

8,615

2,499

3,523

9,190

5,375

1,642

4,871

9,090

1,858

7,329

8,119

Introducing The Lesson:

Tell students that they are going to participate in a Number Roundup, where some numbers actually *are* rounded up—and some are rounded down! After a practice session with the class, students will work in pairs to conduct their own partner roundup.

Steps:

1. Explain the rules for the roundup by reviewing the steps for rounding numbers on page 105.

2. Use the programmed index cards as flash cards for the class to use to practice rounding.

3. Place students in pairs. Give 20 index cards to each pair. Instruct the students to program the cards to match your set.

4. Distribute a copy of page 107 to each student. Explain the directions for completing the reproducible as follows:

    *   Shuffle the index cards and place them facedown in a stack.
    *   Each partner starts with ten points.
    *   Each partner takes a turn drawing a card and rounding the number to the thousands place. He records the number on the reproducible. If he rounds the number up, he adds one point to his score. If he rounds the number down, he subtracts a point from his score.
    *   Play continues until all cards have been used. The winner is the player with the highest score at the end of the roundup.

5. After students have finished the roundup, challenge them to complete the Bonus Box activity.

Name _____

Number Roundup

Follow your teacher's directions for the roundup.
Record your score after each turn.

Number	Rounded to	I rounded up (+1)	down (−1)	Score 10

Bonus Box: Round the year you were born to the nearest tens, hundreds, and thousands places.

How To Extend The Lesson:

- Program several new sets of index cards (or use copies of the pattern below) for the Number Roundup. Place a set of the cards and several blank copies of page 107 in a learning center for student pairs to use.

- Create a daily rounding problem for students to solve at the beginning of each math lesson. For example, challenge students to use the numerals 4, 3, 6, and 8 to write a number that would be rounded to 4,000.

- Place students in pairs for a rounding reinforcement activity. Have each student take a turn rolling a die four times, writing down in order the number shown on each roll. Have the student round the resulting number to the nearest thousand. Instruct the pair to repeat the activity until each partner has rounded ten numbers.

- Reinforce rounding practice with a jar of pennies. Have each student select five pennies and round the date on each coin to the nearest tens, hundreds, and thousands places.

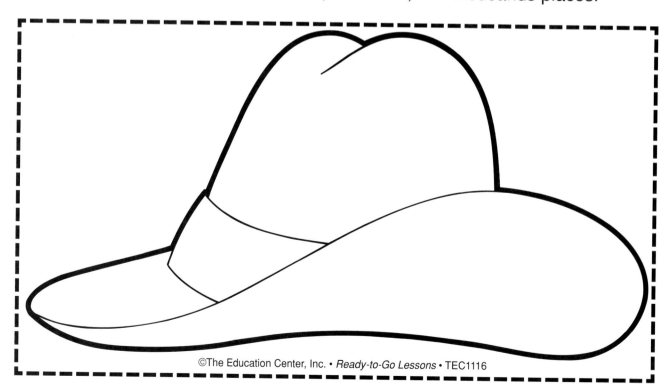

Fraction Sale

Check out these bargain prices for practice in working with fractions!

Skill: Recognizing the fractions of 1/2, 1/3, and 1/4

Estimated Lesson Time: 30 minutes

Teacher Preparation:
Duplicate page 111 for each student.

Materials:
1 copy of page 111 per student

Quick Tip:
Help students remember which number is the numerator and which is the denominator with this reminder:

The **n**umerator is **n**orth of the line.

The **d**enominator is **d**own below the line.

Introducing The Lesson:

Tell students that they are going to practice shopping for bargains with the help of fractions. To demonstrate how to determine a sale price, draw a price tag showing $12 and 12 one-dollar bills below it on the board as shown below. Then tell students that the cost of the item has been marked down. The sale price is one-fourth off the original price. Model the following steps for determining the sale price.

Steps:

1. Group the dollar bills in four equal parts. Explain that each group represents 1/4 of the total amount.

2. Since the sale is for one-fourth off the original amount, cross out one of the groups. Explain that one-fourth of the price has been deducted.

3. Count the remaining dollar bills. Explain that the sale price is the amount left after one-fourth of the total cost was deducted.

4. Repeat the procedure, having students determine the sale price with a discount of one-half and one-third of the $12.

5. Distribute a copy of page 111 to each student. Provide time for students to complete the reproducible.

6. Challenge students to complete the Bonus Box activity.

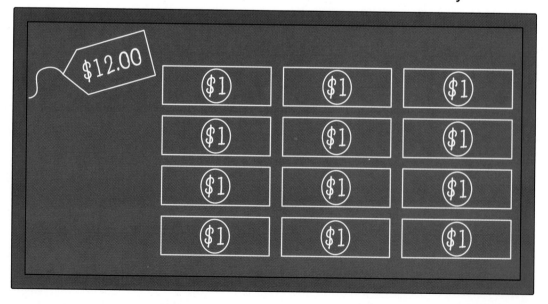

Fraction Sale

Find out the price of each item at the sporting goods sale.

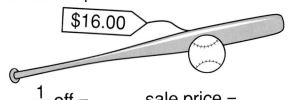

$16.00

$\frac{1}{2}$ off = _____ sale price = _____

 $\frac{1}{4}$ off = _____

sale price = _____

$8.00

 $\frac{1}{4}$ off = _____

sale price = _____

$12.00

$\frac{1}{3}$ off = _____

sale price = _____

$9.00

$10.00

$\frac{1}{2}$ off = _____

sale price = _____

$15.00

$\frac{1}{3}$ off = _____

sale price = _____

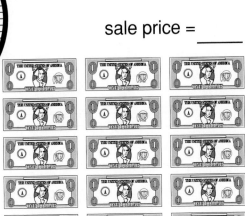

Bonus Box: How much money would you save if you bought every item on sale?

How To Extend The Lesson:

- Give each student an 8" x 8" piece of paper. Have each student fold the paper in half and use a black crayon to visually divide the paper on the fold. Instruct each student to decorate each half of the paper with colored markers or crayons. Glue the completed squares to a butcher-paper backing to create a fraction quilt. Repeat the activity, having students fold their papers into thirds and into fourths.

- Select 12 student volunteers to come to the front of the room. Ask them to arrange themselves in fractional groups, first by fourths, then thirds, and then halves. Repeat the activity with different numbers of student volunteers.

- Have each student draw a picture of a sale item. Instruct the student to include a price tag and the fractional amount that will be deducted. Place the drawings in a learning center with a supply of dollar bills made with the pattern below. Provide time for students to "shop" at the center and determine the sale prices of a specified number of items.

Pattern

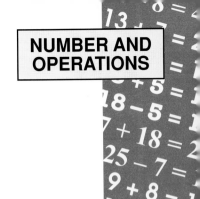

Freewheeling Fractions

*Students will be on a roll with fractions
as they match equivalent amounts!*

Skill: Recognizing equivalent fractions

Estimated Lesson Time: 30 minutes

Teacher Preparation:

1. Duplicate page 115 for each student.
2. Make an overhead transparency of the fraction circles on page 315. Cut out each circle, but do not cut the fractional pieces apart.

Materials:

1 copy of page 115 per student
overhead transparency circles
wipe-off markers
crayons

Teacher Reference:

Share these fraction-related books with your students:
—*Eating Fractions* by Bruce McMillan (Scholastic Inc., 1991)
—*Fraction Action* by Loreen Leedy (Holiday House, Inc.; 1996)
—*Fraction Fun* by David Adler (Holiday House, Inc.; 1996)
—*How Many Ways Can You Cut A Pie?* by Jane Moncure (Child's World, 1987)
—*How Pizza Came To Queens* by Dayal K. Khalsa (Crown Books For Young Readers, 1989)

Introducing The Lesson:

Ask students this riddle: What looks like one-half, is worth the same as one-half, but is not called one-half? The answer is two-fourths! Demonstrate this concept to your students by coloring in two-fourths of a fraction-circle transparency and placing it on top of the fraction circle divided into halves. Show students that both fractions name the same amount.

Steps:

1. Tell students that they will be learning different ways to express equivalent fractional amounts. Demonstrate several equivalent fractions by shading in like amounts of the fraction-circle transparencies with a wipe-off marker.

2. Distribute a copy of page 115 to each student. Provide time for students to color the fraction circles to show equivalent amounts.

3. Challenge students to complete the Bonus Box activity.

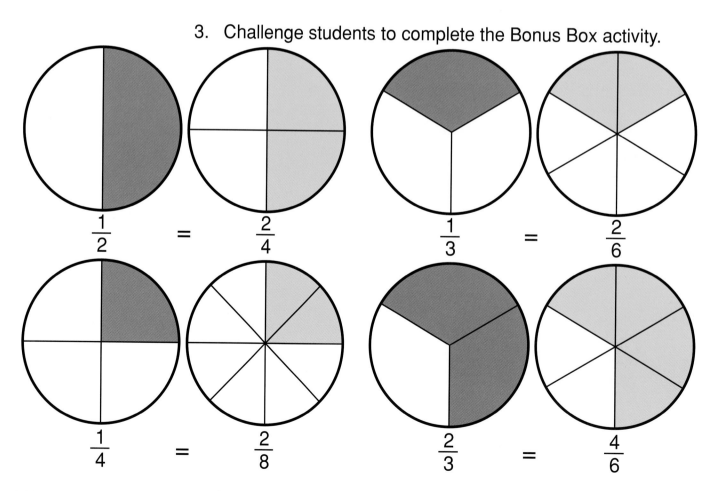

Name_____

Freewheeling Fractions

Color the wheels on each vehicle to show equivalent fractions.
Then write the equivalent fractional amount.

1. $\dfrac{1}{2} = \dfrac{}{4}$

2. $\dfrac{1}{4} = \dfrac{}{8}$

3. $\dfrac{1}{3} = \dfrac{}{6}$

4. $\dfrac{1}{2} = \dfrac{}{6}$

5. $\dfrac{1}{2} = \dfrac{}{8}$

6. $\dfrac{2}{4} = \dfrac{}{8}$

7. $\dfrac{2}{3} = \dfrac{}{6}$

8. $\dfrac{3}{4} = \dfrac{}{8}$

Bonus Box: On another sheet of paper, draw a pizza. Divide it so that eight people would each get one equal slice.

How To Extend The Lesson:

- Provide each student with a ball of clay and a plastic knife. Have each student flatten the ball into a circle, then use the knife to divide it into fractional amounts. Have students compare sizes to determine which fractional pieces are smaller, larger, or equal to each other.

- Play a fraction-recognition game with your students. To prepare for the game, make a spinner from the pattern below. Provide each student with a copy of the fractional circles on page 315. Instruct each student to label the pieces of the circles with their fractional amounts before cutting the circles apart. (If desired, have students color each circle a designated color to help with recognition.)

Play the game as follows:
1. Instruct each student to place the whole circle on his desk.
2. Call out a fraction as determined by the spinner.
3. Each student finds a corresponding piece from his fraction pieces and places it on top of the whole circle.
4. Repeat the process, having students try to cover their circles with the fractional pieces determined by each spin.
5. Players get a point by calling "Trade up!" when two or more pieces can be exchanged for a larger one. Each time a point is earned, make a tally mark on the board.
6. Play until all equivalences have been "traded up" and each student's circle has been covered with two halves. (Note: If the amount of space left to be covered in the circle is smaller than the fraction called, players must wait until the correct fraction is called.)
7. Add up the points. Challenge students to continue play until ten points have been earned.

The Dice Drop

This fast-paced activity will have your students rolling towards success with multiplication!

Skill: Practicing multiplication facts through 6

Estimated Lesson Time: 30 minutes

Teacher Preparation:
1. Duplicate the reproducible on page 119 for each student.
2. Gather the materials listed below.

Materials:
1 copy of page 119 per student
2 dice per student pair (a die pattern is provided on page 92)

Teacher Reference:
Review the following terminology with your students:

Equation: An equation is a sentence that shows that two different numbers or mathematical expressions are equal to each other. An equation uses the equals sign (=), such as in the statement 3 x 4 = 12.

Factor: A factor is a number that is being multiplied. In the equation above, the factors are **3** and **4**.

Multiplication: Multiplication is one of the four basic operations of arithmetic. Multiplication allows you to add the same number a specified number of times. The equation 3 x 4 can also be solved by adding 3 + 3 + 3 + 3, or adding 4 + 4 + 4.

Product: A product is the result of two factors being multiplied. In the equation 3 x 4 = 12, the product is **12**.

Times: Times is another way of saying "multiplied by." The above equation can be read "Three multiplied by four equals twelve," *or* "Three times four equals twelve."

Introducing The Lesson:

Tell students that they are going to work in pairs to roll their way through multiplication practice. Review the terminology on page 117 with your students. Then explain that each pair of students will use two dice to create and solve a set of multiplication problems.

Steps:

1. Distribute a copy of page 119 to each student. Review the directions and demonstrate how to create a problem with a roll of the dice.

2. Place students in pairs to complete the reproducible. Distribute a pair of dice to each set of partners.

3. Each partner will take turns rolling the dice to determine the factors for each multiplication problem. Each partner records the factors on her reproducible, writes a multiplication sentence with the factors, and then finds the product.

4. Provide time for each pair to create ten equations.

5. Challenge students to complete the Bonus Box activity.

The factors are 2 and 4, and the product is 8!

The Dice Drop

Taking turns with your partner, roll the dice five times each.
After each roll, record the numbers shown on the dice as factors.
Write a multiplication sentence with the factors.
Then find the product of the sentence.

Roll Number	Factors	Multiplication Sentence	Product

Bonus Box: Add the products above for a total score. Compare your total with another set of partners.

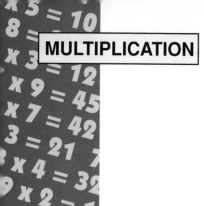

How To Extend The Lesson:

- Arrange students in small groups. Have each group member roll two dice, multiply the numbers together, and then record the product on a sheet of paper. After each group member has had a turn, instruct the members to use the products for these activities:
  —Arrange the products in order from least to greatest.
  —Determine which products are even numbers and which are odd numbers.
  —Find the product with the largest number in the tens place and the product with the largest number in the ones place.
  —Add the products together. Compare to see which group had the largest (or smallest) sum.

- Distribute an index card to each student. Instruct each student to write a numeral from one to six on the card. Call two students to come to the front of the room and show their cards to the class. The first student to say the product of the two numbers earns a point. Play until a student earns five points, or until every student has had the opportunity to earn a point.

- Prepare a bar graph as shown below. Have each student roll two dice and multiply the numbers. Then have her record each product on the appropriate place on the graph.

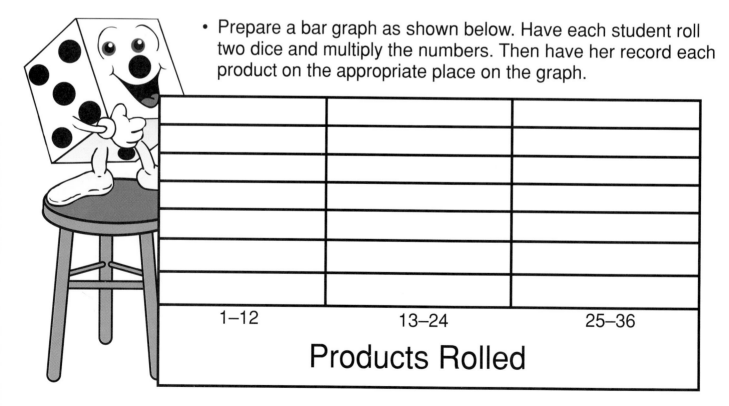

| 1–12 | 13–24 | 25–36 |

Products Rolled

Card Sharks

Multiplication success is in the cards with this fact-reinforcement game!

Skill: Practicing multiplication facts through 10

Estimated Lesson Time: 30 minutes

Teacher Preparation:
1. Duplicate a copy of page 123 for each student.
2. Provide each student with ten index cards or ten 3" x 4" tagboard strips.

Materials:
1 copy of page 123 per student
10 index cards or tagboard
  strips per student
crayons

Quick Tip:
This game can also be played using decks of playing cards instead of programmed index cards. Use a deck of cards for every four students. Give each student one suit of cards. Assign the ace a value of one, and each face card a value of ten. Then have students play the game as described on page 122.

Introducing The Lesson:

Tell students that this math lesson will be a great deal of fun as they work in pairs to play a multiplication card game. Explain that each student will need to follow your directions to create a set of cards to use in the game.

Steps:

1. Distribute ten index cards and a copy of page 123 to each student.

2. Instruct each student to write one numeral from 1 to 10 on each index card.

3. Pair students together to complete the reproducible. To begin, each student places his cards facedown in a stack. Have each partner flip over his top card. The partners use the two numbers as factors for a multiplication problem, which they will write and solve on the reproducible.

4. Have students repeat the steps to create ten problems.

5. Challenge students to complete the Bonus Box activity.

Card Sharks

Follow your teacher's directions to make a set of cards and create ten different
  multiplication problems.

Write and solve each problem on a shark.

Then use the color code to complete the page.

1.

6.

2.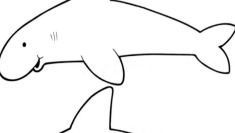

7.

3.

8.

4.

9.

5.

10.

Color the sharks' fins using the following code:

Green   — even-numbered products
Yellow   — odd-numbered products
Red dots — the shark with the greatest product
Blue dots — the shark with the least product

Bonus Box: On another sheet of paper, write the products in order from least to greatest.

How To Extend The Lesson:

• Pair students for a game similar to War using their programmed index cards. The partners sit facing each other with their cards facedown in front of them. On the count of three, each student turns over the top card of his stack and places it in the space between the players. The first student to correctly identify the product of the two numbers wins the round and puts both cards in his stack. Play continues until one student wins all the cards, or until a designated time period is called and students count to see who has collected the most cards.

• Get students moving with a musical-chairs type of activity to practice multiplication facts. To prepare, write a number from one to ten on the board. Instruct each student to select one of her programmed index cards and place it on her desk. At your signal, each student takes a sheet of paper and a pencil and moves to the desk in front of her. The student copies the number from the card on the desk and the number on the board as factors on her paper, then solves the equation. After finding the product, the student waits for your signal to move to the next desk. Continue the procedure until each student has traveled to every desk.

• Use copies of the shark pattern below to program multiplication problems for a learning center activity, or for students to use as flash cards for independent practice.

Playful Pups

Students use problem-solving skills to sort these playful pups by a variety of attributes.

Skill: Sorting

Estimated Lesson Time: 30 minutes

Teacher Preparation:

1. Duplicate page 127 for each student.
2. Gather the materials below.

Materials:

1 copy of page 127 per student
crayons
scissors

Teacher Reference:

Attributes For Creating Student Groups:

- gender
- color of hair
- color of eyes
- number of letters in the student's first name
- number of siblings
- favorite subjects
- age
- types of pets
- transportation to school
- lunch choice

Introducing The Lesson:

Tell the class that they are going to look at different ways to sort things into groups. Ask seven or eight student volunteers to come to the front of the room. Write the word "students" on the board. Explain to the class that the subject of this group is *students,* but if they look closely enough, the class should be able to find a way to divide this group into two smaller categories. Have the seated students observe the group and suggest several ways to divide them into two categories. Possibilities include long-sleeved shirts and short-sleeved shirts, or pants and skirts. Write the names of the two categories under the word "students" on the board. Then challenge students to divide each category into two smaller headings. Record these headings under the appropriate category (see the example below).

Steps:

1. Tell students that each of them will be working with a partner to group a collection of playful puppies.

2. Distribute crayons, scissors, and a copy of page 127 to each student.

3. Pair each student with a partner.

4. Provide time for students to color and cut out the puppies on the reproducible, then complete the sorting activity.

5. Challenge students to complete the Bonus Box activity.

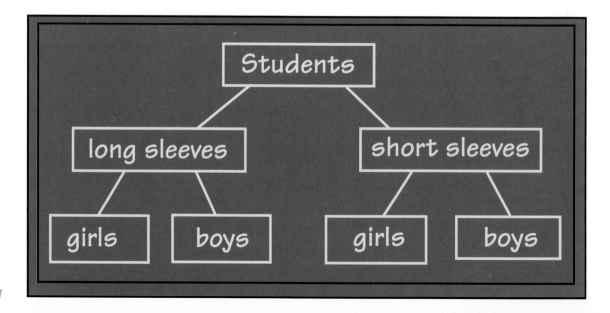

Playful Pups

Color the puppy in each box.
Cut the boxes apart.
Use the puppies in a sorting activity with a partner.

Put both sets of puppy pictures together.
Sort the puppies into two groups. Name these groups.
Then divide each group into two smaller sections. Name each section.
Record the information on the Sort Report.

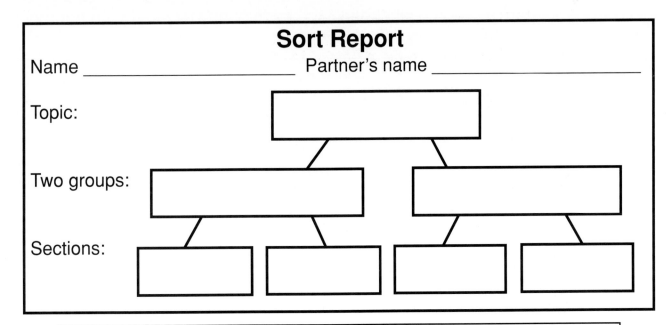

Bonus Box: Put all the puppies together. Sort the puppies in a different way. Record the new information on the back of the Sort Report.

How To Extend The Lesson:

• Have students express the fractional amount of puppies in each section. Remind students that the denominator of each fraction should be 12, since there are 12 puppies all together.

• Have each pair of students arrange the puppy pictures in a bar graph format according to the number of colors on each puppy. Provide a blank bar graph on which students can transfer the information from picture form to recorded data.

• Place students in groups (four or five per group). Have each group decide on a way to sort themselves into two smaller groups, then sort each of these groups into two smaller sections. Have each group stand in front of the class in their sorted arrangement while the class determines the methods of grouping.

• Ask students to bring in spare buttons from home. Store the buttons in a jar and place the jar in a learning center with copies of the Sort Report. A student visits the center, determines a method for sorting the buttons, and records the results on a Sort Report.

• Instruct each pair of students to use two sections as attributes for a Venn diagram. Give each pair two lengths of yarn to fashion into circles for the diagram. Have the students place each puppy picture in the appropriate area of the diagram.

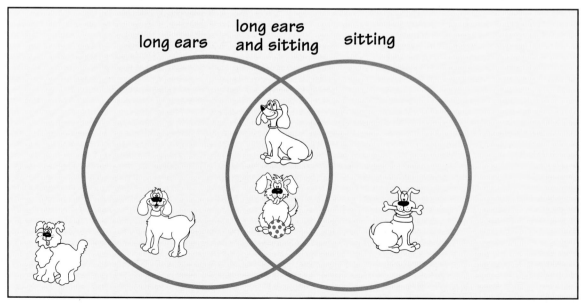

Made To Order

Students put problem-solving and money skills to work as they order from a catalog of toys galore.

Skill: Solving money problems

Estimated Lesson Time: 30 minutes

Teacher Preparation:
1. Duplicate a copy of page 131 for each student.
2. Duplicate a copy of the dollar bills on page 130 for each student.

Materials:
1 copy of page 131 per student
1 copy of the bills on page 130 per student

Teacher Reference:

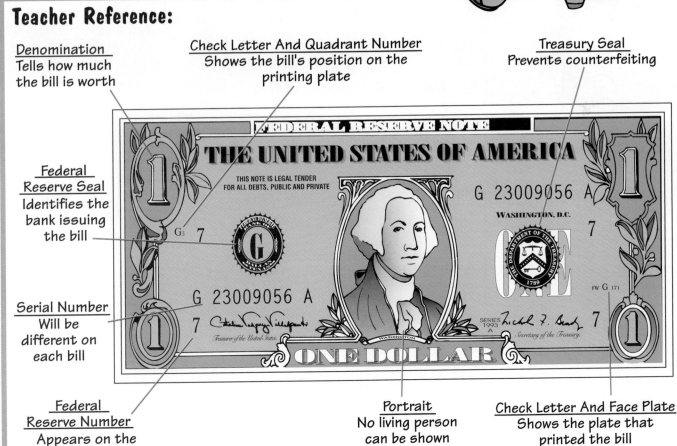

Denomination Tells how much the bill is worth

Check Letter And Quadrant Number Shows the bill's position on the printing plate

Treasury Seal Prevents counterfeiting

Federal Reserve Seal Identifies the bank issuing the bill

Serial Number Will be different on each bill

Federal Reserve Number Appears on the bill four times

Portrait No living person can be shown on U.S. currency

Check Letter And Face Plate Shows the plate that printed the bill

Introducing The Lesson:

Distribute a copy of the bills below to each student. Point out the features of the bills as labeled on page 129. Then tell students that they will "spend" some money as they do a little imaginary shopping from a catalog ad.

Steps:

1. Distribute a copy of page 131 to each student.

2. Allow time for students to list and total purchases within their $10.00 limit (or whatever limit you designate).

3. Challenge students to complete the Bonus Box activity.

Money has been called bread, dough, bucks, clams, moolah, loot, simoleans, and greenbacks!

©The Education Center, Inc. • *Ready-to-Go Lessons* • TEC1116

Made To Order

Place an order from this catalog.
Your teacher will tell you how much money you may spend.
Fill in the order form.
Add to find the total.

Amount of money you may spend: _____

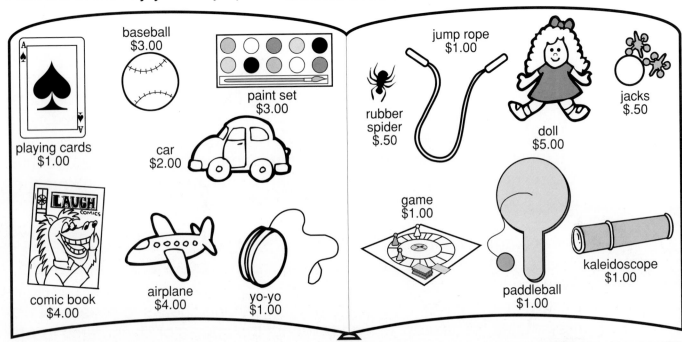

baseball
$3.00

paint set
$3.00

playing cards
$1.00

car
$2.00

comic book
$4.00

airplane
$4.00

yo-yo
$1.00

jump rope
$1.00

rubber
spider
$.50

doll
$5.00

jacks
$.50

game
$1.00

paddleball
$1.00

kaleidoscope
$1.00

Order Form Name of item:	Cost:
Total:	

Bonus Box: Trade papers with a classmate. Check each other's work.

How To Extend The Lesson:

- Collect sale advertisements from newspapers or mail-order catalogs. Have students look through the materials to create a wish list with a predetermined amount of money to "spend."

- Tie in some money-related literature with *Alexander Who Used To Be Rich Last Sunday* by Judith Viorst (Simon and Schuster Children's Books, 1987). Despite his good intentions, Alexander's attempts to save money just never seem to work out. After reading the story, give each youngster a dollar's worth of imitation coins as follows: seven dimes, four nickels, and ten pennies. Reread the story—having students set aside coins as Alexander spends his money. Each time money is spent, have students determine how much money Alexander has left before you continue the story.

- *If You Made A Million* by David Schwartz (Morrow Junior Books, 1994) introduces students to the world of banks, interest, checks, and loans. After reading the story, give each student several copies of the check pattern below. Have the student practice writing checks to several of his classmates. (If desired, assign students the names of classmates to write checks to so that each student receives an equal number.) Collect and distribute the checks to the designated students; then have each student add up the total of his checks.

_____
_____
_____

_____ 20____ 28-8790/2869

Pay To The Order Of _____ $|_____|

_____Dollars

The Best Bank
Sunshine, VA _____
00020

3827344990: 034 876 323 7447

Rock 'n' Roll

Students won't miss a beat as they roll through this partner activity to generate word problems.

Skill: Writing word problems

Estimated Lesson Time: 30 minutes

Teacher Preparation:

1. Duplicate the reproducible on page 135 for each pair of students.
2. Collect two small rocks for each pair of students.

Materials:

1 copy of page 135 per pair of students
2 small rocks per pair of students
1 sheet of 8 1/2" x 11" paper per pair of students

Teacher Reference:

Remind students of some key words for each math operation.

Addition	Subtraction	Multiplication	Division
plus	minus	multiply	divide
all together	subtract	times	for each
add	take away	each	
in all	are left		

Introducing The Lesson:

Tell students that they are going to work in pairs to write and solve word problems. Addition, subtraction, multiplication, or division can be used in this activity.

Steps:

1. Divide students into pairs.

2. Distribute a copy of the Rock 'n' Roll gameboard (page 135) to each pair.

3. Also distribute a piece of paper and two small rocks to each pair.

4. Instruct each pair to follow the directions on the reproducible.

5. Have pairs repeat this procedure until five word problems have been written on their papers.

6. Challenge pairs to complete the Bonus Box activity.

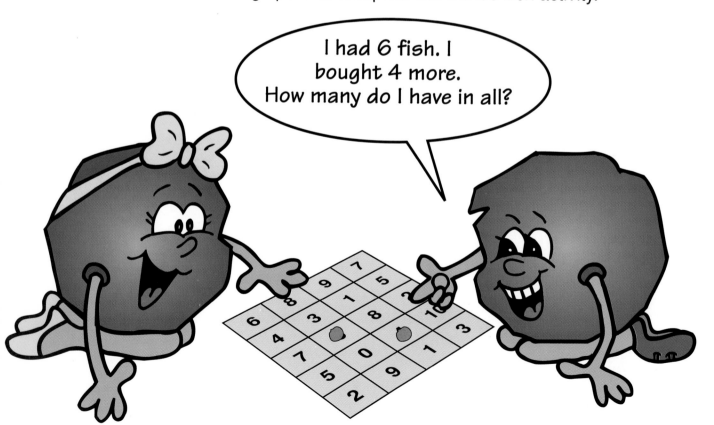

I had 6 fish. I bought 4 more. How many do I have in all?

Name _____

Rock 'n' Roll

Roll your two rocks onto the gameboard.
On the paper, record the two numerals on which they've landed.
Use those two numerals to write a word problem.
Include the answer to the word problem on the back of your paper.

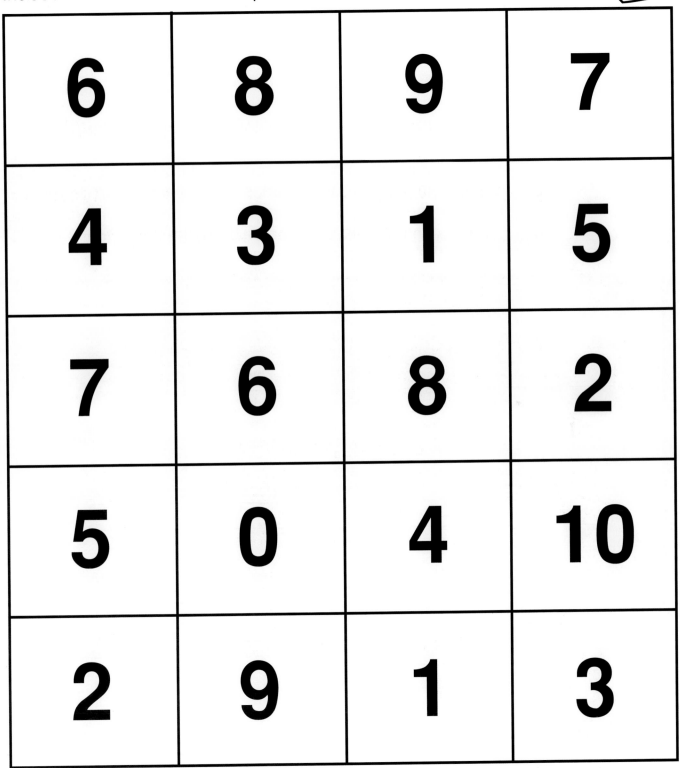

6	8	9	7
4	3	1	5
7	6	8	2
5	0	4	10
2	9	1	3

Bonus Box: Draw a picture that makes sense for each word problem you have written.

How To Extend The Lesson:

- Increase the difficulty level of the activity. Have students reprogram the Rock 'n' Roll gameboard with two- and three-digit numbers and play the game again.

- Give each student a copy of the form below on which to write and illustrate a word problem. Ask him to include the answer on the back of the paper. Collect all the word problems and compile them into a class book titled "Rock 'n' Roll Math."

- Divide students into small groups and have groups develop their own word-problem games. Have each group design a gameboard, write a set of instructions, provide or make needed game components, and demonstrate the game to the class. Store the completed games in a math center.

word problem written by:

Batter Up!

*Have students step up to the plate to choose the operation
for these grand-slam baseball problems.*

Skill: Choosing the operation

Estimated Lesson Time: 40 minutes

Teacher Preparation:
1. Duplicate the reproducible on page 139 for each student.
2. Program six sentence strips as shown below. Fold each strip at the far right edge to hide the operation symbol.

Materials:
1 copy of page 139 per student
6 programmed sentence strips

in all	
all together	+
total	+

how many more ... than	—
how many are left?	—
difference	

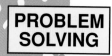

Introducing The Lesson:

Ask your students to volunteer some information about the game of baseball. Record each statement on the board. After a desired number of statements have been recorded, tell students that they will use the information to compose addition or subtraction word problems.

Steps:

1. Use the programmed sentence strips to reinforce key words to look for when determining the operations needed for solving word problems. Show each folded strip to the class and have them determine which operation should be used with each term. Confirm the answer by unfolding the end of the strip to reveal the operation symbol.

2. Challenge each student to compose an addition or a subtraction word problem using information written on the board.

3. Ask student volunteers to share their problems with the class. After each volunteer reads his problem, ask the class to determine which operation is needed to solve the problem.

4. Distribute a copy of page 139 to each student. Provide time for each student to complete the reproducible.

5. Challenge students to complete the Bonus Box activity.

A baseball game has nine innings.
If a batter makes three strikes during his turn at bat, he strikes out.
There are nine field positions.
A baseball is about nine inches around.
A baseball weighs about five ounces.
Regulation bats can't be longer than 42 inches.
There are four bases on the field.
Each base is 90 feet apart.
If a pitcher throws four balls out of the strike zone to a batter, the batter gets to walk to first base.
There are three outs per inning.
A "perfect" game is 27 batters up, 27 batters down—no one makes a hit or gets on base.

Batter Up!

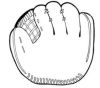

Read each problem.
Decide which operation to use.
Then solve the problem.

	✓ I need to		Answer
	Add	Subtract	
1.			
2.			
3.			
4.			
5.			
6.			
7.			
8.			

1. Myron made 4 hits in the first inning, 2 hits in the second inning, and 2 hits in the fourth inning. How many hits did he make in all?

2. There were 9 batters in the bottom of the third inning. Four batters hit foul balls. How many players did not hit foul balls?

3. In one inning, Pete threw 5 fastballs, 4 curveballs, 7 sliders, and 3 knuckleballs. How many pitches did he throw in all?

4. The Giants scored 11 runs during the game. The Red Sox scored 14 runs. How many runs were scored all together?

5. Bruno had two hits. The first ball traveled 84 feet, and the second ball traveled 79 feet. How many more feet did the first ball travel?

6. A baseball game has 9 innings. So far, 5 innings of a game have been played. How many innings are left to play?

7. The Springfield Sluggers must travel 35 miles to get to Norris Stadium. They must travel 67 miles to get to Rogers Field. How much further do they travel when they play at Rogers Field than at Norris Stadium?

8. During the game, Chavez scored 4 runs, Miller scored 6 runs, and Wilson scored 3 runs. How many total runs did the three players score?

Bonus Box: Lou Gehrig played in 2,130 baseball games without ever missing a game. Find out another fact about a famous baseball player.

PROBLEM SOLVING

How To Extend The Lesson:

- Program an index card for each pair of students with the name of a sport. Have each pair research the sport for statistics and information. Then instruct each pair to write five word problems using the information. Compile the questions into reproducible practice sheets for the class to complete.

- Use a topic of class study for creating word problems. Challenge students to use information from social studies, science, or health lessons to compose several word problems. Provide time during the appropriate subject for students to share their word problems with the class.

- Have students take their places at bat as they select the correct operation for solving word problems. Duplicate a copy of the pattern below for each student. Instruct each student to write an addition sign on one side of the bat and a subtraction sign on the other side. Read several word problems to the class. Have each student hold up her bat to show which operation is needed to solve each problem.

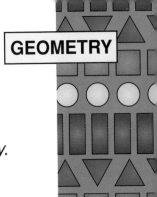

Shape Up!

Reinforce basic geometric shapes with this math-based art activity.

Skill: Identifying geometric shapes

Estimated Lesson Time: 30 minutes

Teacher Preparation:
Duplicate page 143 for each student.

Materials:
1 copy of page 143 per student
crayons (optional)

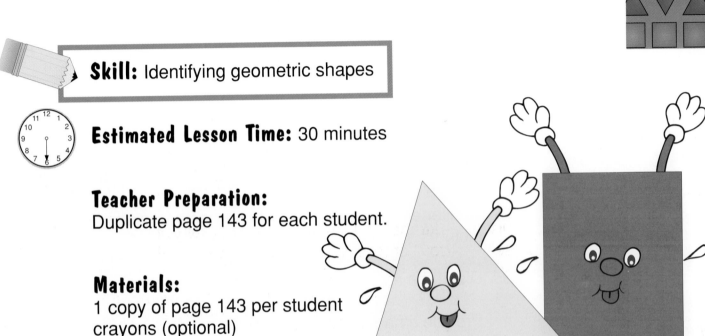

Teacher Reference:

A *circle* is a round, closed figure with all its boundary points the same distance from the center.

An *ellipse* is a closed, oval, plane figure that is not as round as a circle.

A *rectangle* is a plane figure with four straight sides that form right angles.

A *rhombus* is a plane figure with four straight sides of the same length that do not form right angles.

A *square* is a rectangle with four straight sides of equal length that form four right angles.

A *triangle* is a plane figure with three straight sides.

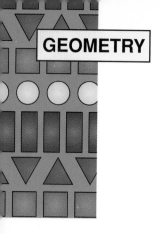

Introducing The Lesson:

Look around the classroom for a few seconds; then announce to your students that you need to get the classroom into shape—or more accurately, shapes. Write the word *circle* on the board. Ask students to name objects in the classroom that are circular in shape. Record their responses on the board.

Steps:

1. Repeat the above procedure to have students name classroom objects that are square, rectangular, and triangular.

2. Challenge students to use these geometric shapes to create pictures.

3. Distribute a copy of page 143 to each student.

4. Provide time for students to draw pictures according to the instructions on the page. If time allows, have students color their drawings.

5. Challenge students to complete the Bonus Box activity.

circle	square	rectangle	triangle
clock	window	paper	shelf
wheel	floor tile	notebook	prism
globe	picture	door	
ball	intercom	computer	
orange			

Shape Up!

Follow the instructions to create a shape picture in each box.

1. Draw a tree.
   Use a rectangle and a circle.

2. Draw a house.
   Use a triangle, a square,
   and four rectangles.

3. Draw a cat.
   List the shapes you used.

4. Draw a robot.
   List the shapes you used.

5. Draw a rocket.
   List the shapes you used.

6. Draw a truck.
   List the shapes you used.

Bonus Box: For each shape, list five objects in your house having that shape.

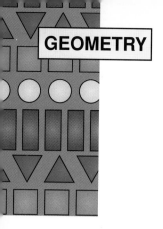

How To Extend The Lesson:

- Enlist the help of your students in creating a collection of objects that represent solid and flat geometric shapes. Place the items—which might include an empty cereal box, a paper-towel roll, an eraser, a pencil, a book, a party hat, a tennis ball, and a box of tissues—in a large box. Invite your students to examine each item and identify it by shape name.

- Have a Shapely Snack Celebration. Encourage students to bring in a supply of snack foods in various geometric shapes. Arrange the snacks on paper plates. Announce the name of a shape; then have each student select one item of that shape. Continue in this manner until all snacks have been taken. Then invite students to munch the tasty shapes.

- Put your class on the lookout for shapes with a mini field trip. Walk around the school grounds and have students find examples of shapes used in floor tiles, brick walls, ceiling tiles, windows, intercoms, and other construction features. Challenge each student to keep a tally-mark record of the different shapes he observes.

- Create abstract works of art by having students cut geometric shapes from wallpaper samples, wrapping paper, or fabric scraps. Instruct each student to arrange and then glue his shapes on a sheet of construction paper. Display the finished projects on a bulletin board with the title "We're Getting Into Shapes!"

WE'RE GETTING INTO SHAPES!

Calculation Carnival

Sharpen estimation skills and review basic math concepts with this small-group activity.

Skill: Estimating; practicing number order, place value, subtraction

Estimated Lesson Time: 45 minutes

Teacher Preparation:

1. Duplicate page 147 for each student.
2. Fill four transparent containers with varied numbers of small objects (dried beans, marbles, dry cereal pieces, math counters).
3. Place each of the containers at a separate numbered station that small groups will visit.

Materials:

1 copy of page 147 per student
4 transparent containers, such as glass jars or plastic cups
4 kinds of small objects to place in the containers (varied number in each container)
4 labels for stations

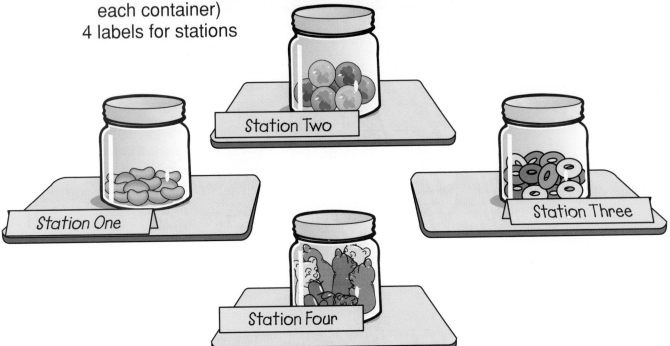

Station Two

Station One

Station Three

Station Four

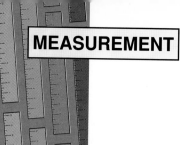
Introducing The Lesson:

Ask students if they have ever been to a carnival. Have students list things they might see at a carnival. Tell them that when you go to a carnival, you like to watch the person at the guessing booth. Ask students if they think they would be good estimators. Hold up one of the transparent containers of objects and ask students to estimate how many objects are in the container. Then ask them to take part in a Calculation Carnival.

Steps:

1. Tell students that they will be working in small groups to estimate the number of objects in the container at each station. After they have made their estimates, each group will complete the rest of the problem-solving activities before moving to the next station.

2. Distribute a copy of page 147 to each student. Divide your class into four small groups, and assign each group to a station for its starting point.

3. Allow time for each group to complete the activities at the first station; then have each group move to the next station in numerical order. Continue in the same fashion until each group has completed all four stations.

4. Challenge each group to complete the Bonus Box activity.

An estimate is a guess at a number. If someone asks you how long it will take you to do your homework and you say, "About an hour," you have made an estimate.

Calculation Carnival

At each station, first estimate the number of objects in the container.
Record your estimate.
Then complete the information for that station.

Station One
- My estimate: _____
- Other estimates in my group: _____ _____ _____ _____ _____
- My group's estimates from least to greatest:

  _____ _____ _____ _____ _____ _____ _____
- The actual number of objects: _____
- The difference between my estimate and the actual number: _____
- The actual number has _____ hundreds, _____ tens, and _____ ones.

Station Two
- My estimate: _____
- Other estimates in my group: _____ _____ _____ _____ _____
- My group's estimates from least to greatest:

  _____ _____ _____ _____ _____ _____ _____
- The actual number of objects: _____
- The difference between my estimate and the actual number: _____
- The actual number has _____ hundreds, _____ tens, and _____ ones.

Station Three
- My estimate: _____
- Other estimates in my group: _____ _____ _____ _____ _____
- My group's estimates from least to greatest:

  _____ _____ _____ _____ _____ _____ _____
- The actual number of objects: _____
- The difference between my estimate and the actual number: _____
- The actual number has _____ hundreds, _____ tens, and _____ ones.

Station Four
- My estimate: _____
- Other estimates in my group: _____ _____ _____ _____ _____
- My group's estimates from least to greatest:

  _____ _____ _____ _____ _____ _____ _____
- The actual number of objects: _____
- The difference between my estimate and the actual number: _____
- The actual number has _____ hundreds, _____ tens, and _____ ones.

Bonus Box: Find the difference between the greatest and least estimate at each station. Write the difference by the group's least-to-greatest information and circle it.

How To Extend The Lesson:

- Use this activity once a week to reinforce estimation skills. Ask students to take turns bringing in small objects to fill the containers.

- Set up a jelly-bean jar. Have each student write his estimate of the number of jelly beans in the jar on a copy of the pattern below. Award the jar to the student with the closest estimation.

- Give each student a small paper cup. Have each student estimate how many pieces of popcorn will fill his cup. Provide popped popcorn, and have each student count the pieces as he fills his cup to check his estimate. Then let students eat the results.

- Expand the numbered stations to include weights. Place a scale at each station and have the group weigh the objects in the container.

- Designate an Estimation Celebration Day. Include appropriate activities throughout the day, such as estimating the number of steps it takes to cross the classroom, the length of a desktop, the height of five math books in a stack, the number of times a student can write his name in one minute, and the number of crackers in a package. Have each student make his estimate, record it on paper, and then complete the activity. Compare the estimates to the actual results.

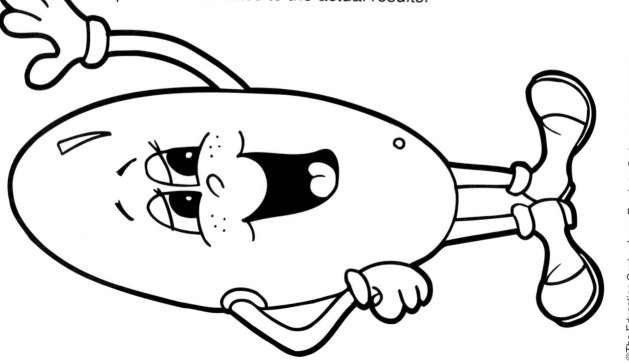

Measurement Quest

*Challenge your class to use both standard and metric units
of linear measurement.*

Skill: Using linear measurement

Estimated Lesson Time: 45 minutes

Teacher Preparation:

1. Duplicate page 151 for each student.
2. Gather the materials listed below.

Materials:

1 copy of page 151 per student
1 ruler with both standard and metric units per student (or use the
   pattern on page 150 to duplicate a class supply)
objects in desks and in the classroom

Teacher Reference:

Ways To Measure Without A Ruler
• a quarter is about 1" wide
• a dollar bill is about 6" long
• many floor tiles are 12" square
• the tip of your pinkie finger is about 1 cm wide
• a nickel is about 2 cm wide

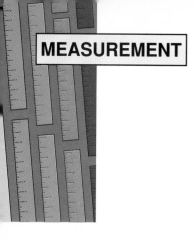

Introducing The Lesson:

Tell students to get ready for a measurement adventure! Ask each of them to look in his desk and find an object about one inch in length. Compare the objects that students have identified.

Steps:

1. Supply each student with a ruler. Ask students to look at the one-inch mark and measure the objects they chose.

2. Tell students that they are going on a measurement search. They will each have a list of lengths and will find an object that is the length of each measurement on the list.

3. Distribute a copy of page 151 to each student.

4. Challenge students to complete the Bonus Box activity.

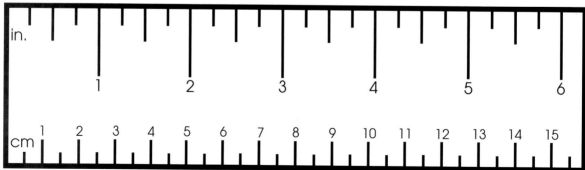

Name_____

Measurement Quest

Use your ruler to draw a line for each of the lengths below.
Find an object in the classroom to match each length.
Write the name of the object above the line you have drawn.

1. 1 inch

2. 4 inches

3. 3 centimeters

4. 6 inches

5. 8 centimeters

6. 2 inches

7. 12 centimeters

8. 7 centimeters

9. 5 inches

10. 15 centimeters

Bonus Box: Measure five items in your desk using both inches and centimeters. Record the items and their lengths on the back of this page.

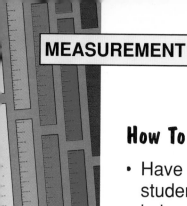

How To Extend The Lesson:

• Have each student create a line drawing with his ruler. Challenge students to include lines ranging from 1 centimeter to 15 centimeters in length.

• Use linear measurement for practice in following directions. Have students listen to your instructions to draw a line three inches long, a box five centimeters square, and other lines and figures.

• Give each student a copy of the form below. Ask students to write their spelling words, then measure the words to see how long they are in inches and in centimeters.

• Supply students with edible manipulatives such as graham crackers, pretzel sticks, or dry cereal. Have students measure them and record the length and width information before eating the treats.

• Create a nonstandard unit of measurement such as the paper clip or an unused crayon length. Have students measure several objects with the new unit and record their lengths and widths.

Spelling word	Length in	
	inches	centimeters
1.		
2.		
3.		
4.		
5.		
6.		
7.		
8.		
9.		
10.		

Terrific Temperatures

Reinforce thermometer skills with temperatures from around the globe.

Skill: Reading a thermometer

Estimated Lesson Time: 30 minutes

Teacher Preparation:

1. Duplicate page 155 for each student.
2. Make an overhead transparency from the pattern on page 154.

Materials:

1 copy of page 155 per student
1 overhead transparency

Teacher Reference:

Some Common Temperatures

Water freezes	32°F	0°C
Water boils	212°F	100°C
Room temperature	70°F	20°C
A moderate oven	350°F	175°C
A cold day	20°F	−10°C
A warm day	85°F	30°C

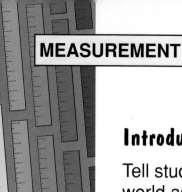

Introducing The Lesson:

Tell students that they will be looking at temperatures from around the world as they practice recording data on a thermometer. Inform students that they will be looking at average temperatures from the month of January. Ask students to name some average winter temperatures for your region.

Steps:

1. Show students an overhead transparency of the thermometer on the bottom of this page. Point out the two-degree increments between each number. Use a wipe-off marker to show students how to record a temperature on the thermometer.

2. Have students practice recording some local winter temperatures on the transparency.

3. Distribute a copy of page 155 to each student. Provide time for students to complete the reproducible.

4. Challenge students to complete the Bonus Box activity.

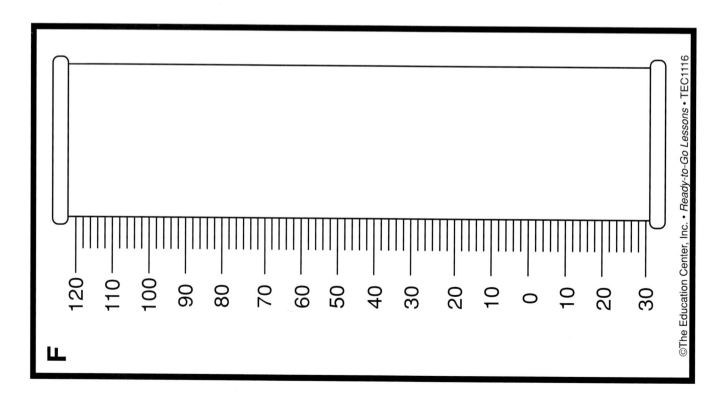

©The Education Center, Inc. • *Ready-to-Go Lessons* • TEC1116

Name_____

Terrific Temperatures

Read the sentence below each thermometer.
Find the information on the chart.
Then record each temperature in the blank and on the thermometer.

January Station	Average Daily Temperatures	
	High	Low
Athens, Greece	54	42
Berlin, Germany	35	26
Bombay, India	88	62
Capetown, South Africa	78	60
Copenhagen, Denmark	36	29
Hong Kong, China	64	56
Lima, Peru	82	66
Oslo, Norway	30	20

1.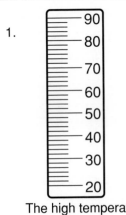
The high temperature for Oslo, Norway, is ____°F.

2.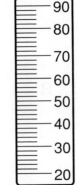
The low temperature for Lima, Peru, is ____°F.

3.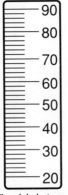
The high temperature for Copenhagen, Denmark, is ____°F.

4.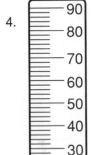
The low temperature for Athens, Greece, is ____°F.

5.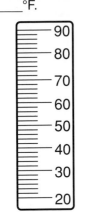
The high temperature for Capetown, South Africa, is ____°F.

6.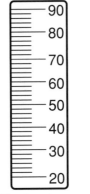
The low temperature for Bombay, India, is ____°F.

7.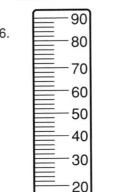
The low temperature for Berlin, Germany, is ____°F.

8.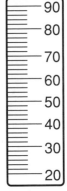
The low temperature for Hong Kong, China, is ____°F.

Bonus Box: On another sheet of paper, draw a thermometer showing your favorite temperature.

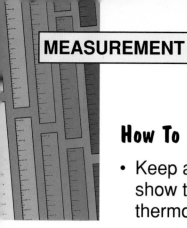

How To Extend The Lesson:

• Keep a daily record of the high temperature. Have a student volunteer show the temperature each day on an enlarged, laminated copy of the thermometer pattern on page 154.

• Have students research to find the average monthly high and low temperatures for your region. Then have students use the data to find out which month has the coldest temperatures, the warmest temperatures, the greatest amount of difference in temperature, and the least amount of difference in temperature.

• Discuss with your students the effect temperature has on the plants and animals of a region. Have students research to find which plants and animals prefer warmer climates and which prefer colder climates.

• Have students keep a record of the low temperatures for a week. Then have students use the information to create a class line graph. For an added challenge, ask students to also record the high temperatures and add the information to the graph with a different color.

• Share the following temperature-related literature with your students:
  —*Fifty Below Zero* by Robert Munsch (Annick Press, 1986)
  —*The Science Book Of Hot & Cold* by Neil Ardley (Harcourt Brace Juvenile Books, 1992)
  —*Temperature* by Brenda Walpole (Gareth Stevens, Inc.; 1995)
  —*Weather Forecasting* by Gail Gibbons (Simon & Schuster Children's Books, 1993)

Wally's Watch

Students will use time-telling skills to answer these problems like clockwork

Skill: Telling time to the quarter hour

Estimated Lesson Time: 30 minutes

Teacher Preparation:

1. Duplicate the reproducible on page 159 for each student.
2. Gather a supply of face-clock manipulatives, or make copies of the patterns on page 316.

Materials:

1 copy of page 159 per student
1 clock manipulative per student

Teacher Reference:

Discuss these timely sayings with your students:

- Time flies.
- In the nick of time
- A stitch in time saves nine.
- The time of your life
- Time out
- Time is money.
- In the right place at the wrong time
- Wasting time
- For the time being
- Time's on your side.

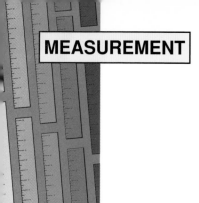

Introducing The Lesson:

Tell students that your friend Wally the Moose is always early for everything because his watch is 15 minutes fast. Explain that if it is really 12:00, Wally's watch will read 12:15. Use a manipulative face clock to show 12:00; then demonstrate how to count by fives to 15 while moving the minute hand ahead 15 minutes. Tell students that they will practice determining what time Wally's watch will read.

Steps:

1. Distribute a manipulative clock to each student. Instruct each student to position the hands so that the clock reads 12:00. Then count together as everyone moves the minute hand so that the clock reads 12:15.

2. Have students continue guided practice. Announce a starting time for the clocks, and have students determine what Wally's watch would read by moving the minute hand 15 minutes ahead. Continue with several examples until students have understanding.

3. Distribute a copy of page 159 to each student. Provide time for students to complete the reproducible.

4. Challenge students to complete the Bonus Box activity.

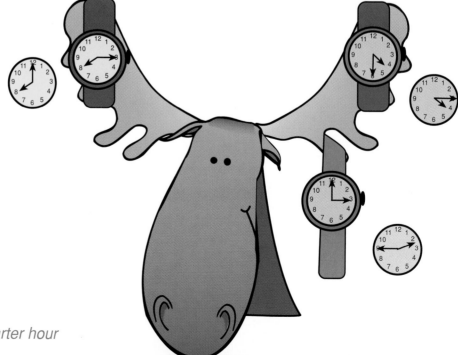

Wally's Watch

Wally's watch is set 15 minutes fast.
Look at the clock that shows the real time.
Write the real time, and then tell what time Wally's watch
   would show.

Example:
The real time is __3:00__ .
Wally's watch would show __3:15__ .

---

1. 

Time to call
Mama Moose!

The real time is _____ .
Wally's watch would show _____ .

2.

Meet Morris
for a movie.

The real time is _____ .
Wally's watch would show _____ .

3.

Brush teeth and get
ready for bed.

The real time is _____ .
Wally's watch would show _____ .

4.

Moose Scouts
meeting!

The real time is _____ .
Wally's watch would show _____ .

5.

Remember to watch
"Moose On The
Loose."

The real time is _____ .
Wally's watch would show _____ .

6.

Don't forget the
wildlife tour!

The real time is _____ .
Wally's watch would show _____ .

7.

Appointment to
polish antlers.

The real time is _____ .
Wally's watch would show _____ .

8.

Time to get a
new watch!

The real time is _____ .
Wally's watch would show _____ .

Bonus Box: Tell what time Wally's watch would show when school starts, when you go to lunch, and when school is over.

How To Extend The Lesson:

- Make a class clock with your students. Have 12 students sit in a circle to represent the numbers on a clock face. Place one student in the middle of the circle and give her two sentence strips—a long one to represent the minute hand, and a shorter one to represent the hour hand. Call out times to the quarter hour and have students position the hands to show the times.

- Throughout the day, assign students various tasks that will take 15 minutes to complete. At the beginning of each activity, instruct students to write down the starting time and predict what the ending time will be. Then have students read silently, solve a set of math problems, write spelling words, or work on another assignment for 15 minutes. When time is up, have students write down the ending time and compare it to their predictions.

- Use the digital clock pattern below to have students practice reading digital times as well as analog times.

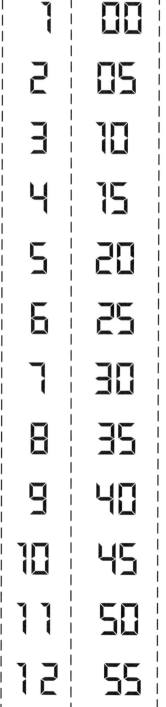

1	00
2	05
3	10
4	15
5	20
6	25
7	30
8	35
9	40
10	45
11	50
12	55

ALARM

HOUR SET   MINUTE SET

ON
Off

From Time To Time

Provide practice with time-telling skills as students try their hands at creating clock faces.

Skill: Telling time to five minutes

Estimated Lesson Time: 30 minutes

Teacher Preparation:

1. Duplicate a copy of page 163 for each student.
2. Write a different digital time on each of ten index cards.
3. Place the index cards inside a large envelope.
4. Duplicate the clock pattern on page 316, or use a face-clock manipulative.

Materials:

1 copy of page 163 per student
10 programmed index cards
1 large envelope
1 face-clock manipulative

Teacher Reference:

Test your students' concepts of time with these time trivia questions:

- How many hours are in one day?
- How many minutes are in one hour?
- How many seconds are in one minute?
- What hours are A.M. times?
- What hours are P.M. times?
- When is it noon?
- When is it midnight?
- What does the term "half past the hour" mean?
- What does the term "quarter past the hour" mean?
- Which seems longer—an hour of homework, or an hour of free time?

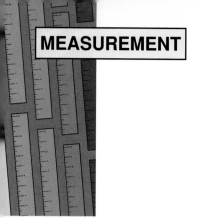

Introducing The Lesson:

Tell students that they are going to use their ability to count by fives to practice telling time. Remind students that each number on the clock represents a five-minute increment. Touch each number on the clock while counting by fives to review with students how to read the minute hand.

Steps:

1. Set the clock manipulative for 1:15. Ask students to identify the hour and minutes shown on the clock.

2. Have students read several other times on the clock for guided practice.

3. Distribute a copy of page 163 to each student. Tell students that you will show them cards with digital times written on them. Each student will draw hands on a clock face to correspond with each card.

4. Select one card at a time from the envelope. Show the card to your students and provide time for them to draw hands corresponding with its digital time.

5. After students have completed the reproducible, challenge them to complete the Bonus Box activity.

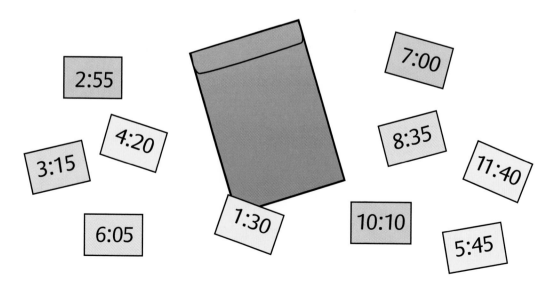

From Time To Time

Draw the hands on each clock face as your teacher shows you a digital time.

1.

6.

2.

7.

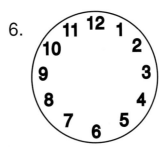

3.

8.

4.

9.

5.

10.

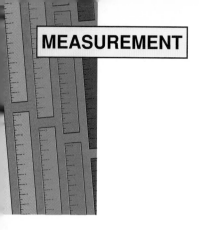
How To Extend The Lesson:

- Repeat the activity after programming another set of index cards. Or, if you prefer, have each student program one index card. Collect the cards and use them with the activity.

- Challenge students to complete the activity in reverse. Put ten pictures of standard clocks in the envelope. Show one clock at a time to your students and have them write the digital time on a sheet of paper.

- Ask students to predict several tasks that they think can be accomplished in five minutes. How many spelling words do they think they can write in five minutes? How many pages could they read? After students have made predictions, try the activities and discuss the results.

- Have students make their own sandglasses to practice time-telling skills. Collect the necessary materials and have each student follow the instructions below for constructing a sandglass.

Materials
Each student will need:
2 empty, plastic two-liter bottles—well rinsed and dried
packing tape
2 cups of sand
access to a funnel
access to a clock with a second hand

1. Use the funnel to pour the sand into one of the bottles.
2. Tape the second bottle to the first one as shown.
3. Look at the second hand of a clock. When the hand reaches the 12, invert the sandglass and determine how long it takes for the sand to pour from one bottle to the other.

- Afterward, ask students to predict how much sand it would take to make a one-minute timer, a two-minute timer, and a five-minute timer. For an added challenge, ask students to think of a way to slow down the flow of sand from one bottle to the other.

Our Favorite Things

From raindrops on roses to whiskers on kittens, students will make dazzling discoveries as they graph a collection of class favorites.

Skill: Creating a bar graph

Estimated Lesson Time: 40 minutes

Teacher Preparation:

1. Duplicate page 167 for each student.
2. Provide a bag of jelly beans or other multicolored candy. Each student will need one piece of candy (but have extras so each student will not be limited when choosing his favorite color).

Materials:

1 copy of page 167 per student
1 bag of jelly beans or another candy (1 candy per student plus extras)
crayons

Teacher Reference:

A Dozen Things To Graph

How many…
- people are in your family?
- pets do you own?
- buttons do you have on?
- cousins do you have?
- letters are in your name?
- trees are in your yard?
- pockets are you wearing?

What's your favorite…
- TV show?
- sandwich?
- sport?
- song?
- planet?

Introducing The Lesson:

Tell your students that this lesson will show their favorites! Hold up the bag of jelly beans or other colored candies. Ask each student to select one piece of his favorite color of candy.

Steps:

1. Tell students that you notice many different favorites. Explain that a good way to record information about students' favorites is to create a graph. Ask students to identify their favorites from such topics as ice-cream flavors, cartoon shows, and sports.

2. Write each of three topic titles on the board. Have each student name his favorite under each topic as you record his responses on the board.

3. Distribute a copy of page 167 to each student.

4. Divide students into three groups and assign each group a topic from the board to graph. Have each group complete page 167 together.

5. Challenge students to complete the Bonus Box activity.

ice-cream flavors	cartoon shows	sports
I mint chocolate chip	III Rocket Ranger	III football
III cookies-'n'-cream	THL Detective Dawg	THL basketball
THL rocky road	III Rags Rabbit	IIII soccer
II cherry vanilla	III Silly Squid	II baseball
THL strawberry	II Farmer Fox	II tennis

Name _____

Our Favorite Things

Write the name of the topic as the title of your
  graph.
Write one of the favorites from the board below
  each column.
Color the graph to show which choices are favorites in
  your class.

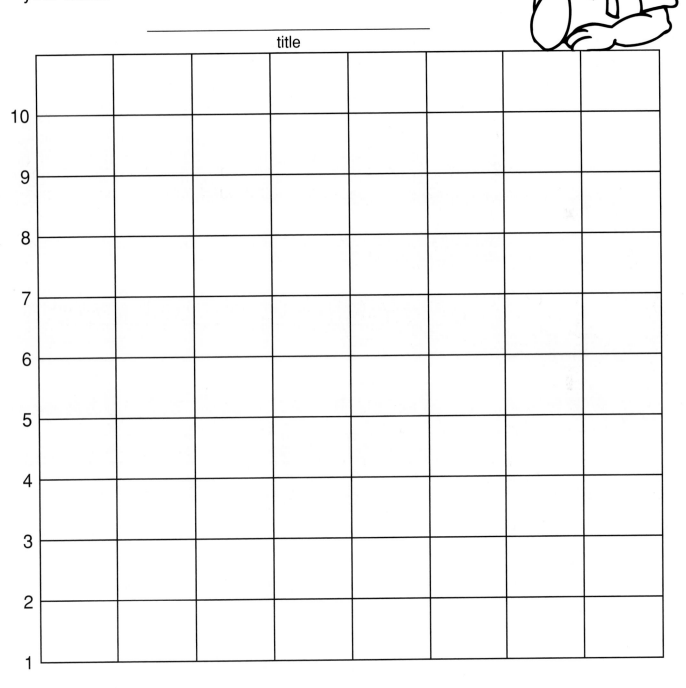

_____
title

10
9
8
7
6
5
4
3
2
1

___ ___ ___ ___ ___ ___ ___

Bonus Box: On the back of this paper, draw a picture to show which choice had the most
boxes colored in.

How To Extend The Lesson:

• After reading a story, have each student decide on her favorite character. Have the class make graphs to show the results.

• On each Friday, ask students to choose which cafeteria lunch was their favorite that week. Have students graph the results.

• Ask each student to wear a shirt of her favorite color to school on a certain day. Make a human graph by having students stand in lines according to their shirt colors.

• Have each student take a copy of page 167 home and make a graph of items in his favorite room of his house. If desired, help students program the columns with common items—such as chairs, tables, beds, windows, and lamps—or send home a note asking a parent to help the child program this graph. Have students bring the resulting graphs back to school and share the information.

• As each student completes an extension activity, reward her with a copy of the award pattern below.

The results are in...
and when it comes to graphing,
You're GREAT!

To:_____ From:_____

Cat, Dog, Fish, Frog... What's The Most Popular Pet?

Conduct a class survey to determine the favorite type of pet; then have your students graph the results.

Skill: Creating a line graph

Estimated Lesson Time: 40 minutes

Teacher Preparation:

1. Duplicate the reproducible on page 171 for each student.
2. Provide a sheet of paper for each student to use as a tally sheet, or duplicate a class supply of the tally sheet on page 172.

Materials:

1 copy of page 171 per student
1 sheet of paper or tally sheet per student

Teacher Reference:

Questions To Follow Up A Graphing Activity

1. Which column had the most?
2. Which column had the least?
3. How many more are in column ___ than in column ___?
4. What is the total of column ___ and column ___?
5. Are any columns the same?
6. Which two columns have the greatest difference?
7. How many total responses were there?
8. What statements could be made using the results of the graph?

Introducing The Lesson:

Tell your students that they will gather information to find out which type of pet is most popular with their classmates. After gathering the information, each student will record the results on a line graph.

Steps:

1. Distribute a sheet of paper or a copy of the tally sheet to each student. Show students how to list each category and how to record a tally mark for each response.

2. Have each student stand and name the type of pet(s) she has at home. Assist students in making tally marks in the correct place on their tally sheets as each response is made. As different types of pets are named, it may be necessary for students to list new categories.

3. After each student has had a turn, ask the class to total the tally marks for each category on their tally sheets.

4. Distribute a copy of page 171 to each student. Show the students how to set up categories for the graph to match the information on their tally sheets.

5. Show students how to transfer the information from their tally sheets to the line graph by placing a dot on the appropriate line.

6. After students have completed their graphs, challenge them to complete the Bonus Box activity.

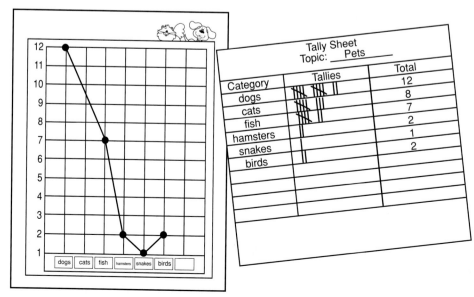

Name_____

Cat, Dog, Fish, Frog...What's The Most Popular Pet?

Use the results of your tally sheet to construct a line graph.

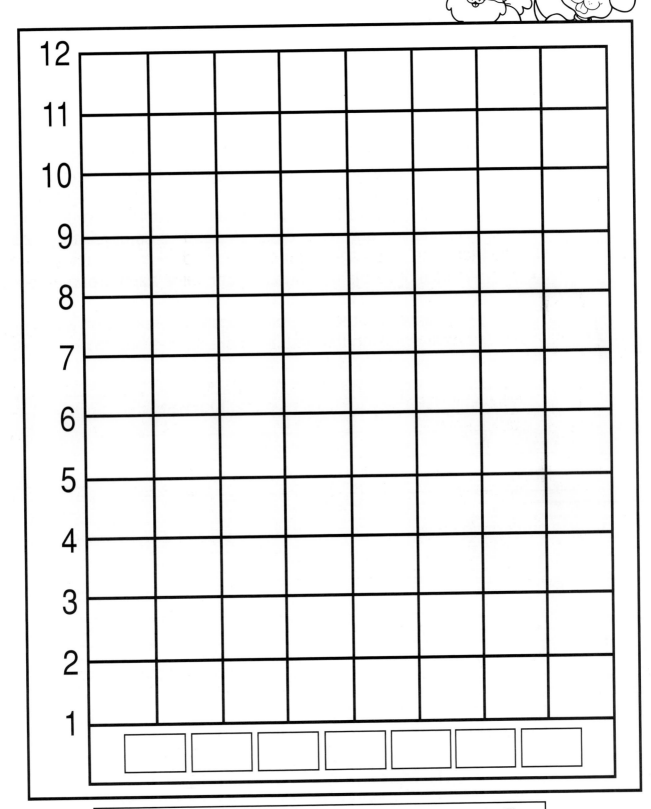

Bonus Box: On another sheet of paper, tell which pet is most popular. Then list three reasons why it is a popular pet.

How To Extend The Lesson:

- Have each student conduct another survey with the tally sheet, then graph the results on a copy of the line-graph form. Students can survey to find out the class's favorite color, day of the week, holiday, or type of pizza; or students may wish to create their own survey questions.

- Reinforce comparison skills by having students work in pairs to survey different classrooms. Decide on a question for the survey. Assign each student pair a classroom to interview. Have the pair record the results on a line graph. Then post the completed line graphs and ask students to compare the findings.

- Place students in groups of four. Give each group a bag of colored candies or fruit snacks. Ask each group to sort the different flavors in the bag, then record the results on a line graph. After graphing the results, invite each group to equally divide the pieces and enjoy a snack!

Tally Sheet		
Topic:_____		
Category	Tallies	Total

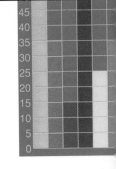

Incredible, Edible Circle Graphs

Have your students create and compare circle graphs.
Then eat the results!

Skill: Creating a circle graph

Estimated Lesson Time: 30 minutes

Teacher Preparation:

1. Duplicate the reproducible on page 175 for each student.
2. Provide a brown, paper lunch bag for each group of four students.
3. Place a cup of colored, fruit-flavored cereal pieces (such as Froot Loops®) in each bag.

Materials:

1 copy of page 175 per student
1 brown, paper lunch bag for each group
colored, fruit-flavored cereal
crayons

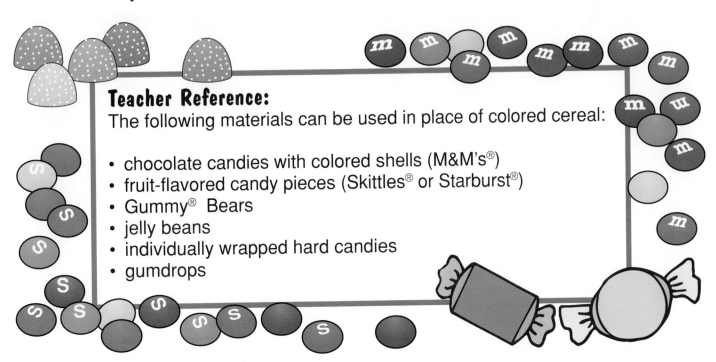

Teacher Reference:

The following materials can be used in place of colored cereal:

- chocolate candies with colored shells (M&M's®)
- fruit-flavored candy pieces (Skittles® or Starburst®)
- Gummy® Bears
- jelly beans
- individually wrapped hard candies
- gumdrops

Introducing The Lesson:

Tell your students that they will be constructing a special graph to record information about a tasty topic. Students will work in groups to gather information, record data, and compare results about fruit-flavored cereal pieces.

Steps:

1. Distribute a copy of page 175 to each student.

2. Place students in groups of four. Provide each group with an assortment of crayons and a brown, paper lunch sack containing a cup of fruit-flavored cereal pieces.

3. Instruct each group member to reach into the bag without looking and select eight pieces of cereal. Have her arrange the pieces on the appropriate section of the reproducible, placing like colors side by side.

4. After each child has had a turn, have students color the graphs to show the results of each group member.

5. Instruct students to write a statement under each graph.

6. Challenge students to complete the Bonus Box activity.

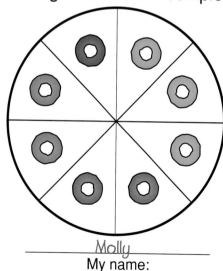

Molly
My name:
A statement about the graph:
There are the same amount
of red and blue pieces.

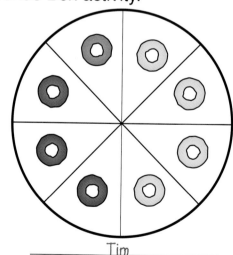

Tim
My name:
A statement about the graph:
There are more yellow
pieces than any other color.

Incredible, Edible Circle Graphs

Follow your teacher's directions to complete the graphs below.

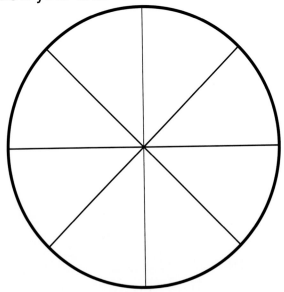

My name: _____
A statement about the graph:
_____
_____

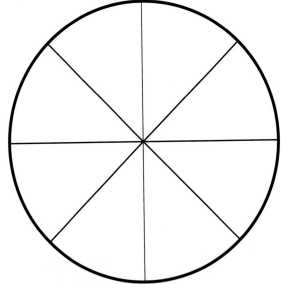

Group member's name: _____
A statement about the graph:
_____
_____

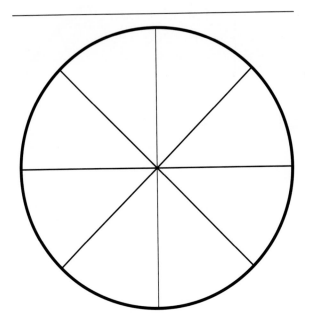

Group member's name: _____
A statement about the graph:
_____

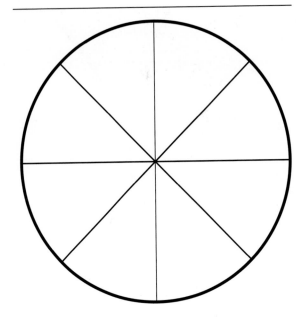

Group member's name: _____
A statement about the graph:
_____

Bonus Box: On another sheet of paper, tell which colors were picked most often and least often. Then write two other conclusions about the graphs.

How To Extend The Lesson:

- Provide each group with another copy of the reproducible and a penny. Instruct each student to flip the coin eight times and record the number of heads and tails on a circle graph. After each group member has had a turn, have the students compare the results.

- Reinforce fractional numbers as you discuss the graphs. Have each student make a statement about the graph using fractions to describe the results.

- Distribute a copy of the ten-section circle graph below to each student. Instruct each student to think of a survey topic, such as favorite colors, to chart on the graph. Provide time for students to collect data from their classmates, then show the results on their graphs.

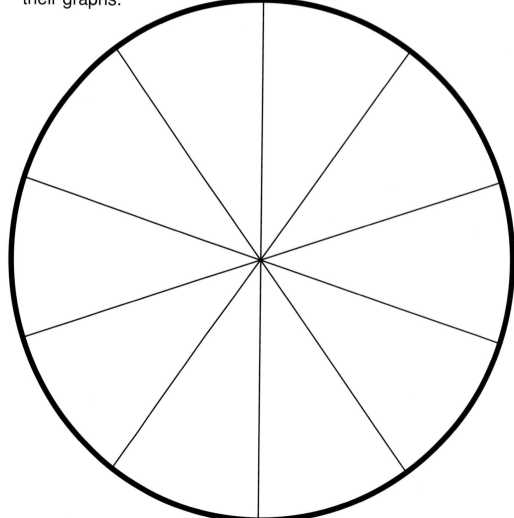

©The Education Center, Inc. • *Ready-to-Go Lessons* • TEC1116

What Changes

Investigate the life cycles of several different species with this fascinating activity.

Skill: Exploring life cycles

Estimated Lesson Time: 45 minutes

Teacher Preparation:
Duplicate page 179 for each
   student.

Materials:
1 copy of page 179 per student
one 3" x 12" construction-paper
   strip per student
scissors
stapler
crayons

Background Information:
All living organisms have a cycle of life. Exaqmples of two animal life cycles are as follows.

Frog Life Cycle:
A female frog lays hundreds of eggs. A tadpole hatches. Hind legs develop, followed by the developing of the tadpole's lungs and its front legs. Then the tadpole loses its gills, and a tiny frog—still with a stump of a tail—emerges from the water. Finally, the frog absorbs its tail and can live out of the water.

Butterfly Life Cycle:
A female butterfly deposits an egg on a leaf. A caterpillar, or *larva,* hatches. The caterpillar munches on leaves and outgrows its skin, molting, four or five times. Next the caterpillar stops eating and attaches itself to a twig or leaf. Then it molts for the final time, and a chrysalis, or *pupa,* is exposed. Finally a butterfly emerges from the chrysalis.

Introducing The Lesson:

Ask students to raise their hands if they have ever seen pictures of themselves when they were babies. Invite student volunteers to share what they looked like and how they were able to survive (since they couldn't walk, talk, or take care of themselves).

Steps:

1. Review with students the four stages of the human life cycle—baby, child or teen, adult, and senior citizen. Ask students to think about people who are in these different stages of their lives.

2. Remind students that animals, like humans, have life cycles too. Use the Background Information on page 177 to share the life cycles of a frog and a butterfly.

3. Distribute a copy of page 179 and a construction-paper strip to each student. Have each student color and cut out the cards. Next have him set the four title cards aside, then sort the remaining cards into four stacks of life cycles: ant, owl, frog, and butterfly.

4. Next have the student sequentially number each set of cards (in the provided circles), then place each title card on top of its corresponding stack. Finally have the student staple each stack to the construction-paper strip as shown.

5. After students have completed their projects, have each child write a brief description of each animal's life cycle.

6. Encourage students to use their completed projects to share their knowledge of life cycles with their families.

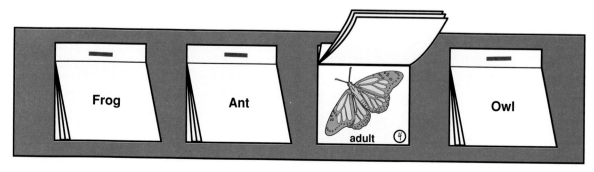

adult	larva	egg	chick
egg	adult	caterpillar	young owl
young frog	egg	adult	egg
tadpole	pupa	chrysalis	adult
Frog	**Ant**	**Butterfly**	**Owl**

How To Extend The Lesson:

- Have students investigate the life cycles of other animals. To do this have each student choose a different animal to research. Provide a variety of arts-and-crafts materials for students to use in creating diagrams about the life cycles they researched. Some ways students might choose to show their information:

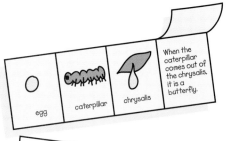

  —**Life-cycle flip books:** To make a book for a four-stage life cycle, a student folds a 12" x 18" sheet of drawing paper in half (to 6" x 18") and makes three equally spaced cuts in the top layer. Then she sequentially labels and illustrates the four resulting flaps with the desired life cycle. Next she lifts each flap and writes a description of the stage.

  —**Four-panel drawings:** A student folds a sheet of drawing paper into fourths, unfolds it, and labels each section with one of the four life-cycle stages. Then in each section she describes and illustrates a stage of the life cycle.

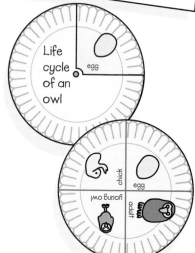

  —**Life-cycle wheels:** A student divides each of two paper plates (or nine-inch tagboard circles) into four equal sections. She labels and illustrates the top-right quadrant on one plate with the first stage of the life cycle. Then she rotates the plate one-quarter turn clockwise, and labels and illustrates this quadrant with the second stage. She continues in the same manner for the remaining two stages. To make a wheel cover, she cuts away one section of the other plate and personalizes the plate as desired. Then she uses a brad to attach the wheel cover atop the wheel. To share her project, she turns the bottom plate clockwise.

- Share the following life-cycle literature with your students:
  —*Butterfly Story* by Anca Hariton (Dutton Children's Books, 1995)
  —*Tale Of A Tadpole* by Barbara Ann Porte (Orchard Books, 1997)
  —*The Life And Times Of The Honeybee* by Charles Micucci (Houghton Mifflin Company, 1997)
  —Life Cycles series by Sabrina Crewe (Raintree Steck-Vaughn Publishers)

Awesome Adaptations

Explore the wonders of animal adaptations with a look at some fascinating features!

Skill: Identifying animal adaptations

Estimated Lesson Time: 30 minutes

Teacher Preparation:
1. Duplicate page 183 for each student.
2. For each student, program a slip of paper with a different animal name from the list on page 182.
3. Prepare a sign for each of the following habitats: wetlands, drylands, woods, and grasslands. Mount each sign on a different classroom wall.

Materials:
1 copy of page 183 per student
1 programmed slip of paper per student
4 signs, each programmed with the name of a
   habitat (wetlands, drylands, woods, grasslands)

Background Information:
In order to survive, animals must compete with other animals in their living environments, or *habitats*. Animals have special features to help them find food, shelter, and protection. The list below describes some of the special features, or *adaptations,* that allow certain animals to survive.

frog—long, sticky tongue for catching insects
elephant—long trunk for reaching leaves
raccoon—long, flexible fingers for grabbing prey
duck—webbed feet for swimming and diving
eagle—hooked beak and long, curved talons for
   catching prey
bee—thick, hairy legs for collecting pollen
shark—many rows of sharp, replaceable teeth for
   catching prey

bat—high-pitched sound waves *(echolocation)* for
   finding insects
pelican—long, straight bill with a flexible pouch for
   catching fish
anteater—long, slender snout and a long tongue for
   reaching into anthills
spider—ability to spin webs for catching insects
squirrel—powerful jaw muscles and sharp front teeth
   for gnawing through hard-shelled nuts
snake—jaw that can open wide for swallowing whole prey

Introducing The Lesson:

To begin, tell students that they will place animals in their *habitats,* or living environments. Read aloud and point to the mounted habitat signs. Then distribute a programmed slip of paper to each student. Have each student read the animal name on her paper and then stand in its corresponding habitat.

Steps:

1. Have the students in each habitat display their animal names to each other to verify that each student is in the correct area. Collect the paper slips and randomly redistribute them, making sure everyone receives a new slip. Then repeat the activity. Continue in the same manner for a desired amount of time.

2. After the students return to their seats, inform them that each animal has special *adaptations,* or features to help it survive in its habitat. Share the Background Information on page 181 with your students. Then ask student volunteers to identify adaptations of the animals on their paper slips.

3. Distribute a copy of page 183 to each student for her to complete.

4. Challenge students to complete the Bonus Box activity.

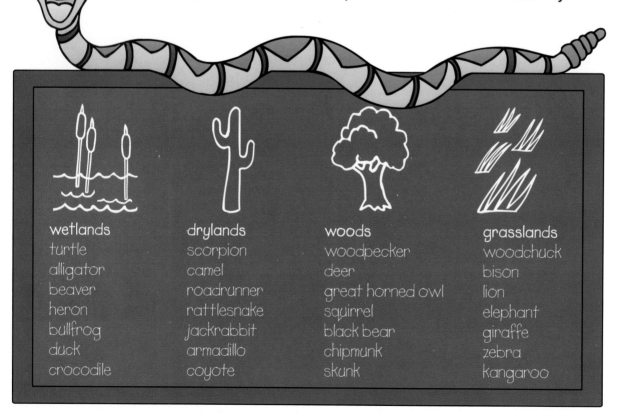

wetlands	drylands	woods	grasslands
turtle	scorpion	woodpecker	woodchuck
alligator	camel	deer	bison
beaver	roadrunner	great horned owl	lion
heron	rattlesnake	squirrel	elephant
bullfrog	jackrabbit	black bear	giraffe
duck	armadillo	chipmunk	zebra
crocodile	coyote	skunk	kangaroo

Awesome Adaptations

Animals have special features, or *adaptations*, to help them find food, shelter, and
   protection.
Read each sentence.
Write the matching word on the line.
Use the Word Bank.

Bonus Box: Choose an animal not in the Word Bank. On the back of this sheet, describe how this animal finds food, shelter, and protection.

1. An _____ has a long snout for reaching into anthills.

2. A _____ has webbed feet for swimming and diving.

3. A _____ spins a web to trap insects.

4. A _____ can stretch its jaw to swallow its prey whole.

5. A _____ has many rows of replaceable teeth to catch and eat its prey.

6. A _____ has hairy legs that collect and transport pollen.

7. A _____ uses high-pitched sounds to find insects.

8. An _____ has sharp talons to kill and carry prey while flying.

9. A _____ has a sticky tongue to catch insects.

10. An _____ has a long trunk for reaching tree leaves.

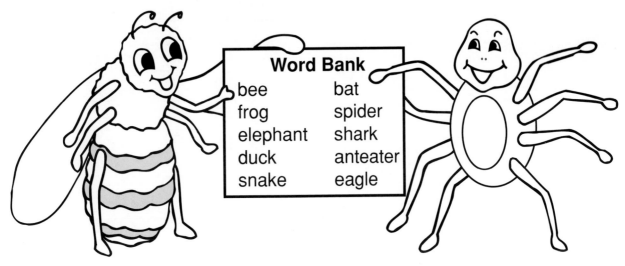

Word Bank

bee	bat
frog	spider
elephant	shark
duck	anteater
snake	eagle

How To Extend The Lesson:

- Have each student select an animal from the lesson to research. Encourage each student to prepare an oral report, a poster, or a fact sheet about the animal of her choice.

- From discarded magazines have students cut out pictures of animals and mount each picture on a tagboard square. Place the pictures at a center, and have students sort and categorize them by habitats, survival attributes, types of animals, or eating habits.

- Inspire your students to create imaginary animals. To do this, have each student decide on the distinctive features of two different animals. Instruct the student to draw a picture of an animal with those features combined. To extend the activity, have the student write a paragraph describing his creature. Display the completed projects on a bulletin board for all to enjoy.

Here Come The Vertebrates!

Teach your students to identify vertebrates with a lesson that has a lot of backbone!

Skill: Classifying vertebrates

Estimated Lesson Time: 45 minutes

Teacher Preparation:
1. Duplicate page 187 for each student.
2. Make a chart or overhead transparency of the vertebrate list shown below.

Materials:
1 copy of page 187 per student
1 prepared chart or overhead transparency
one 9" x 12" sheet of light-colored construction paper per student
crayons or markers
scissors
ruler
glue

Background Information:
A *vertebrate* is an animal with a backbone. Four main groups of vertebrates are *mammals, fish, birds,* and *reptiles.* The chart below shows important information for identifying the majority of creatures in each group.

Mammals	Birds	Fish	Reptiles
• warm-blooded	• warm-blooded	• cold-blooded	• cold-blooded
• have lungs	• have lungs	• have gills	• have lungs
• have hair or fur	• have feathers	• have scales	• have scaly skin
• live birth	• lay eggs	• live birth or lay eggs	• live birth or lay eggs
• most care for young	• most care for young	• most do not care for young	• most do not care for young

Introducing The Lesson:

Ask each student to put one hand on his back and feel his backbone. Have students try arching their backs, curving their backs, sitting up straight, and turning from side to side while feeling their backbones. Introduce the word "vertebrate" by writing it on the chalkboard. Tell students that animals with backbones are called vertebrates. Ask students if they think they belong to that group.

Steps:

1. Display a chart or overhead transparency of the Background Information on page 185. Discuss the information with your students.

2. Demonstrate how to create four columns on a 9" x 12" sheet of construction paper by folding the paper twice and then unfolding it. Instruct each student to write "Vertebrates" at the top of his paper and then use a ruler to draw columns as shown. Next have him label each column with a different animal group: "Mammals," "Birds," "Reptiles," and "Fish."

3. Distribute a copy of page 187 to each student. Have each student color and cut out the animal cards, then glue each card under the corresponding heading.

4. Display the completed projects in the classroom for students to refer to during your study of animals.

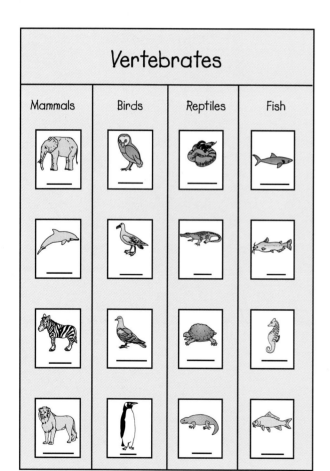

Animal Cards

Use with Step 3 on page 186 and the first extension idea on page 188.

elephant	**owl**	**snake**	**catfish**
shark	**Gila monster**	**seagull**	**zebra**
pigeon	**seahorse**	**dolphin**	**crocodile**
carp	**lion**	**turtle**	**penguin**

How To Extend The Lesson:

- Provide practice identifying vertebrates with an indoor game similar to Four Corners. Label each corner of your classroom with one of the animal groups discussed in the lesson (mammal, fish, reptile, and bird). Duplicate a copy of page 187, cut out each animal card, and place the cards in a container. Count to ten as each student walks to the corner of her choice. Randomly select an animal picture from the container. The students standing in the corner labeled with the group to which that animal belongs must sit down. Continue play until only one student is left. (When four or fewer students are playing, each player must select a different corner.) Declare the winning player the Victorious Vertebrate; then play another round!

- This nifty idea reinforces the fact that people are vertebrates, too! Distribute crayons and a three-inch, white construction-paper circle to each student. Have each student design a badge to wear that will remind or inform others that people are vertebrates. Encourage students to write messages such as "I'm proud to be a vertebrate!" or "Hooray for vertebrates!" on their badges. Pin the badges to (where else?) the back of the students' shirts.

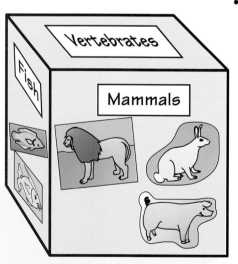

- Have students use a large cardboard carton to create a display showcasing the four groups of vertebrates from the lesson. Cover the carton with bulletin-board paper, and label each of the four sides (not including the top and the bottom) with one of the following groups: mammals, fish, reptiles, and birds. From discarded magazines have students cut out pictures of animals belonging to each group. Instruct students to glue each picture to the appropriate side of the box. For a finishing touch, create a sign labeled "Vertebrates" for the top of the carton.

What Fascinating Creatures!

In this partner activity, students will learn astonishing facts about a variety of Earth's creatures!

Skill: Recalling facts about animals

Estimated Lesson Time: 30 minutes

Teacher Preparation:
Duplicate a construction-paper copy of page 191 for each student pair.

Materials:
1 construction-paper copy of page 191 per student pair
1 resealable plastic bag per student pair
1 pair of scissors per student pair

Background Information:
Fascinating facts about eight creatures:
- **cricket**—Not all animals have ears on their heads. A cricket has ears on its knees.
- **honeybee**—A honeybee tells other bees where to find food by performing a waggle dance in a figure eight. This dance tells the other bees how much food there is and where to fly to find it.
- **anteater**—An anteater can collect 500 ants with one lick.
- **prairie dog**—Prairie dogs kiss when they meet to find out if they are from the same group. If they are, they groom each other. If not, they fight, and the intruder is driven away.
- **lizard**—If a lizard's tail is broken off, the lizard can usually grow a new one.
- **flamingo**—A flamingo is pink because its body takes on the pink color of the shrimp it eats.
- **elephant**—An elephant spends 23 hours a day eating.
- **fly**—A fly takes off backwards.

Introducing The Lesson:

Ask each student to think about something fascinating about herself. Examples might include a time when she jumped rope for one full minute or that she can do a split. Invite volunteers to share their thoughts. Then tell students that many animals have interesting habits or characteristics that they will learn about today.

Steps:

1. Pair students; then give each pair a construction-paper copy of page 191.

2. Share the Background Information on page 189 with your students while they find the picture of each creature on the reproducible.

3. Instruct one student in each student pair to cut apart the cards on the reproducible. Then have each twosome place the cards facedown to play a Concentration-type game. Explain the rules of the game as follows:

   • In turn each student selects two cards to flip over. If the cards make a match of a picture and its corresponding information, the student keeps the two cards and takes another turn. If the cards do not produce a match, the player returns them to the facedown position and the second player takes a turn.

   • Play continues until all cards have been matched. The player with the most pairs wins the game.

4. If time allows, pair each student with a different partner to play another round of the game.

5. Have student pairs store their cards in resealable plastic bags for future use.

A cricket has ears on its knees.	A honeybee tells other bees where to find food by dancing.	An anteater can collect 500 ants with one lick.	When two prairie dogs meet, they kiss to find out if they're from the same group.
cricket	**honeybee**	**anteater**	**prairie dog**
If a lizard's tail is broken off, the lizard can usually grow a new one.	A flamingo is pink because its body takes on the pink color of the shrimp it eats.	An elephant spends 23 hours a day eating.	A fly takes off backwards.
lizard	**flamingo**	**elephant**	**fly**

I'm a bird that can turn my head around far enough to see behind me. Who am I?

an owl

How To Extend The Lesson:

- Encourage your students to further re-search the creatures listed in the lesson. Have each student select one of the creatures and design a shoebox di-orama showing the animal in its natural habitat. Display the completed projects in the classroom or library for a fiercely fascinating exhibit.

- Challenge your students to find fascinat-ing facts about animals not listed in the lesson. As each student discovers an in-teresting fact about a creature, have him create a picture card and fact card to add to the ones used in the game de-scribed on page 190. Store the game cards in a learning center for students to use during free time or for review purposes.

- Use interesting facts about animals as a springboard for a writing project. Pro-vide reference materials on a variety of animals, and instruct each student to discover intriguing information about the creature of her choice. Challenge the student to use the information to write a riddle about the animal. To do this, a student writes her riddle on one side of a sheet of drawing paper, then flips her paper and illustrates the answer on the back. Compile the completed pages into a class riddle book titled "Amazing Ani-mal Information."

State Your Matter

*Capitalize on students' knowledge of solids,
liquids, and gases to create a class guessing game.*

Skill: Classifying the states of matter

Estimated Lesson Time: 45 minutes

Teacher Preparation:

1. Duplicate page 193 for each student.
2. For each student pair, write a different setting on a slip of paper. Settings might include a birthday party, a movie theater, the beach, and an amusement park.

Materials:

1 copy of page 193 per student
1 programmed slip of paper per student pair
1 piece of writing paper per student pair

Background Information:

• All matter takes up space and has weight.
• The three physical states of matter are *solid, liquid,* and *gas.*
• The physical properties of matter include its size, shape, color, weight, taste, and smell.

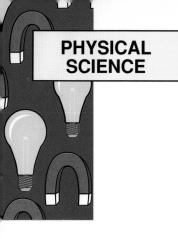

Introducing The Lesson:

Tell your students that each one of them has something in her kitchen that can change from a solid, to a liquid, to a gas. Ask students to try to name the substance. After several responses, confirm that the answer is water. It can take the form of a solid (ice), a liquid (water), or a gas (steam).

Steps:

1. Ask each student to imagine the kitchen in her home. Write the words "solids," "liquids," and "gases" on the chalkboard. Ask students to list items found in their kitchens. Write their responses under the appropriate headings.

2. Explain to students that they will work in pairs to brainstorm and categorize states of matter found in various settings. Then they'll use their ideas in a class guessing game.

3. Pair students; then give each twosome a sheet of writing paper and a slip of paper that has been labeled with a particular setting. On the writing paper, have each pair list items found in its setting.

4. Next distribute a copy of page 195 to each student. Have each student write the items from her and her partner's list in their corresponding categories. Then have her use the resulting information to complete the two questions at the bottom of the reproducible.

5. After students complete their reproducibles, have each student pair share its items for each state of matter. Challenge the remaining students to guess the setting. Continue in this manner until all the twosomes have shared their items.

Things Found In The Kitchen

solids

crackers

bread

table

chair

liquids

water

milk

juice

oil

gases

air

steam

nonstick spray

State Your Matter

Read the setting written on your slip of paper.
Brainstorm with your partner different items found in the setting.
Write the items in the correct box.

The Setting: _____

Solids	**Liquids**	**Gases**

Answer.

1. What could be found in your setting that might not be found in another setting?

    _____

    Is it a solid, liquid, or gas? _____

2. Would you find more matter in a solid, liquid, or gas state at your setting?

    _____

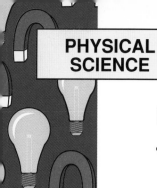
How To Extend The Lesson:

• Supply each student with a paper lunch sack that has a solid object placed inside. On a sheet of paper, have each student write clues about the object in her bag and tell about its physical properties. Ask each student to read aloud her clues and have classmates guess what is hidden inside her bag.

• Divide a bulletin board into three sections labeled "solids," "liquids," and "gases." Have students look through discarded magazines and newspapers to find pictures of the different states of matter. Then have each student pin his pictures on the bulletin board in the correct section.

• Have students categorize the school lunch menu into solids and liquids. Then challenge each student to create her own lunch menu that includes both solids and liquids. To do this, a student folds a sheet of construction paper in half, opens it, and writes her lunch choices inside. Then she decorates the front cover of the menu as desired. Encourage students, in turn, to read aloud each item on their menus and have their classmates name whether it is a solid or a liquid.

vegetable soup (liquid)

apple (solid)

roll (solid)

grilled cheese sandwich (solid)

milk (liquid)

Check Out The Changes!

Help students investigate changes in matter with this high-interest activity.

Skill: Identifying changes in matter

Estimated Lesson Time: 30 minutes

Teacher Preparation:
Duplicate page 199
for each student.

Materials:
1 copy of page 199
   per student
1 piece of scrap paper
   per student

Matter Man

Background Information:

Matter is anything that takes up space. It can take
the form of a solid, liquid, or gas. Matter can change in two ways:

- **Physical changes** usually cause a difference in the look or feel of matter, but
  the molecules that make up the matter stay the same. When a piece of paper is
  crumpled, it may look different, but it is still paper. Physical changes can include
  variations in color, texture, size, shape, and form (solid, liquid, or gas).
- **Chemical changes** result in the matter's molecules being altered to form a new
  substance. When a piece of paper is burned, it becomes ash. It is no longer
  paper. Chemical changes occur when matter is burned, rusted, or spoiled (as
  with food).

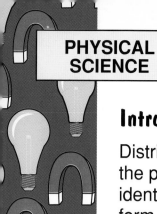

Introducing The Lesson:

Distribute a piece of scrap paper to each student. Remind students that the paper is a form of matter because it takes up space. Ask students to identify which form of matter the paper is—a solid, liquid, or gas. Then inform your students that there are often changes in matter, which they will help you demonstrate.

Steps:

1. Have each student crumple his paper into a ball. Ask students to list some of the changes they observe. (It changed size and shape.) Reinforce to students that the paper, although changed in appearance, is still paper.

2. Share the Background Information on page 197 with your students.

3. Then tell students that if you burned a piece of paper, that would result in a chemical change. Reinforce that after being burned, the paper is no longer paper. It would change size, shape, color, texture, and substance.

4. Reinforce that crumpling the paper would cause a *physical* change, whereas burning it would cause a *chemical* change.

5. Distribute a copy of page 199 to each student. Provide time for students to read about and identify each type of change described.

6. Challenge students to complete the Bonus Box activity.

Physical Changes

water that has frozen

paper that has been torn

wood that has been cut

Chemical Changes

paper that has burned

metal that has rusted

food that has spoiled

Name _____

Check Out The Changes!

When matter changes only in the way it looks or feels, it is a *physical* change. When matter changes to become a new substance, it is a *chemical* change.

Read about each physical or chemical change in matter. Answer each question.

Matter Man

1. You crumple a paper bag into a ball.

   What changes happen? _____

   Is the bag still a bag? _____

   Is this a physical or chemical change? _____

2. You burn an old letter into many pieces.

   What changes happen? _____

   Is the letter still a letter? _____

   Is this a physical or chemical change? _____

3. You cut a sandwich in half.

   What changes happen? _____

   Is the sandwich still a sandwich? _____

   Is this a physical or chemical change? _____

4. A metal toy is left in a puddle of water, and it rusts.

   What changes happen? _____

   Is the metal still a metal? _____

   Is this a physical or chemical change? _____

5. A picture fades after being in the sunlight.

   What changes happen? _____

   Is the picture still a picture? _____

   Is this a physical or chemical change? _____

Bonus Box: On the back of this paper, draw pictures to show how a candle, a crayon, and a scoop of ice cream can each be changed.

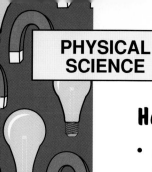

How To Extend The Lesson:

- Assist your students in completing these simple experiments to observe changes in matter. Distribute copies of the form below for students to use to record their observations.

  —Place one sheet of colored construction paper in a bright, sunny window and another sheet of the same color in a closet. After three days compare the differences in the two papers.

  —Place one iron nail in a cup of water for a week and one iron nail in an empty cup. Remove the nail from the water, and compare it with the nail that was kept dry.

  —Cut an apple in half and leave the halves exposed to the air for several hours. Cut another apple in half, and compare the freshly cut pieces with those that were left out.

  —Place a piece of chalk and a crayon in separate cups of water. After several hours observe any changes in each object.

  —Place a rock, a cotton ball, and an apple slice in the freezer overnight. The next day observe any changes in each object.

Form

Name _____ Recording sheet

Check Out These Changes!

Test conditions: _____

Objects tested:

Object 1 _____

Object 2 _____

Object 3 _____

What changes occurred?

Object 1 _____

Object 2 _____

Object 3 _____

Matter Man

It's Simply Simple Machines!

*Take your students on a school tour in search of
the six types of simple machines.*

Skill: Identifying simple machines

Estimated Lesson Time: 45 minutes

Teacher Preparation:
1. Duplicate page 203 for each student.
2. Gather the materials listed below.

Materials:
1 copy of page 203 per student
2 crayons per student
1 textbook per student
1 ruler per student
1 pencil per student
1 clipboard or book per student

Background Information:
There are six different simple machines that help people work.

- **Lever:** A stiff bar that rests on a support (or fulcrum). It lifts or moves loads.
- **Wheel And Axle:** A wheel with a rod (axle) going through its center. Both parts work together to lift or move loads.
- **Pulley:** A grooved wheel with a rope or cable around it. It moves things up, down, or across.

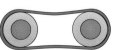

- **Inclined Plane:** A slanting surface used to connect a lower surface to a higher surface. Objects move up or down on it.
- **Wedge:** An object with at least one slanting side that ends in a sharp edge. It cuts or splits an object apart.
- **Screw:** An inclined plane wrapped around in a spiral. It holds things together or lifts.

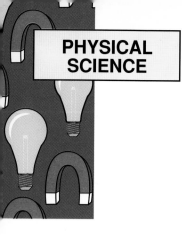

Introducing The Lesson:

Tell students that they are going to work with machines today—simple machines. Explain that a machine does not have to be a complicated contraption with many parts powered by electricity. In fact all complex machines are based in some way on six types of simple machines. Simple machines make work easier. To observe a simple machine in action, each student will need two crayons and a textbook.

Steps:

1. Have each student place the textbook on the left side of her desk. Instruct her to move it to the right by pushing on it. Ask students if they can feel the *friction* of the book against the desk.

2. Next have each student place two crayons underneath the book. Have each student try moving the book again, this time with the aid of two crayon "wheels" under the book. Explain to students that a *wheel* is a machine that makes work easier.

3. Have students observe another example of a simple machine. Tell each student to place one of the crayons by the edge of her textbook. Instruct the student to roll the crayon to the top cover of the book.

4. Distribute a ruler to each student. Have each student place the ruler on the edge of the book to make a ramp. Tell students to roll their crayons up the ramps to get to the top covers of the books. Explain that the ruler acted as another simple machine, an *inclined plane,* to make the work easier.

5. Share the Background Information on page 201 with your students. After describing the six different simple machines, tell students that they will go on a walking tour around the school in search of simple machines.

6. Distribute a copy of page 203 to each student. Instruct the student to take the paper, a pencil, and a clipboard or book (to use as a writing surface) on the walking tour.

7. Walk with your students around the school grounds as they look for and record examples of simple machines.

8. Back in the classroom, challenge students to complete the Bonus Box activity.

Did your students find some of these simple machines around your classroom or school?

Lever: seesaw, hammer claw, shovel
Wheel And Axle: wagon, rolling pin, car, book cart
Pulley: flagpole, window blinds, stage curtains
Inclined Plane: slide, wheelchair ramp
Wedge: plastic knife, nail, fork, plastic needle
Screw: water faucet, jar lid, fan, plastic bolt

Name _____

It's Simply Simple Machines!

Simple machines make work easier for us.
Look for examples of the simple machines labeled in the boxes.
Write the examples that you find.

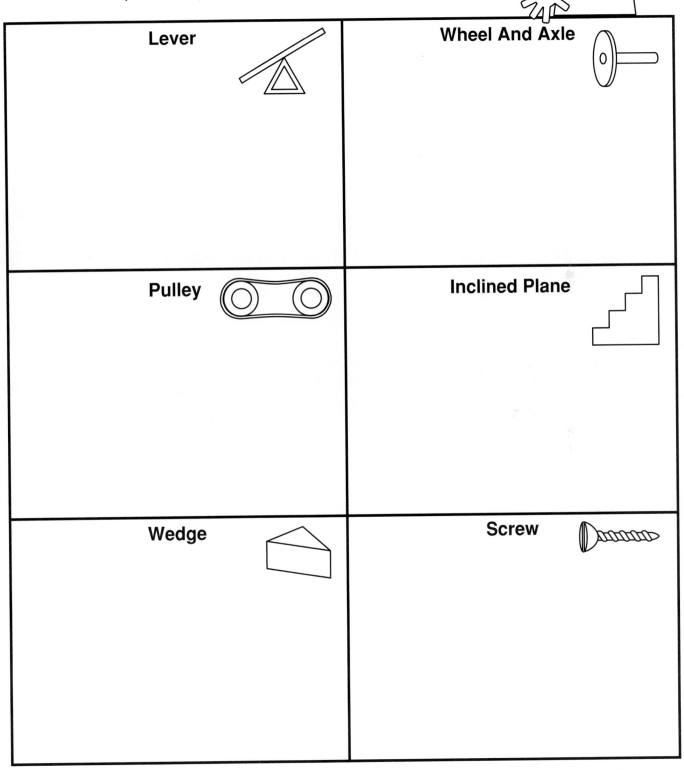

Lever	Wheel And Axle
Pulley	**Inclined Plane**
Wedge	**Screw**

Bonus Box: On the back of this paper, draw an example of each of three simple machines you have at home.

How To Extend The Lesson:

- Have students create posters recognizing the six simple machines. To begin divide students in six small groups and assign each group a different simple machine. Provide each group with a sheet of poster board, glue, scissors, and discarded magazines. Instruct each group to look through the magazines for examples of its assigned simple machine. Have each group cut out and glue its findings to the poster board; then display the completed creations for the class to refer to during your study of simple machines.

- Incorporate creative writing into your study of simple machines. Distribute a sheet of drawing paper to each student. Have the student design an invention using two or more simple machines, then write a paragraph describing the invention and what it does. Provide time for students to share their creations with the class.

- Reinforce the six simple machines with a game of Concentration. Pair students and distribute 12 index cards to each pair. Instruct the twosome to write the name of a different simple machine on each of the first six cards, then list an example or draw a picture of each of the corresponding machines on the remaining six cards. Have the partners shuffle the completed cards and place them facedown. In turn each student turns over two cards, trying to match a simple machine name with its example or picture. If a match is made, the student keeps the cards and takes another turn. If the cards do not match, the student returns them to their positions, facedown, and his partner takes a turn. Play continues until all cards have been matched. The student with the most cards wins!

Looking Into Light

Fascinate your young scientists with this enlightening lesson on light!

Skill: Identifying transparent, translucent, and opaque objects

Estimated Lesson Time: 30 minutes

Teacher Preparation:
Duplicate page 207 for each student.

Materials:
1 copy of page 207 per student
1 translucent object, 1 opaque object, and 1
    transparent object (See examples listed below for suggestions.)
flashlight (optional) or another light source

Background Information:
- Light travels in a straight line when nothing is in its way. When the light is blocked, it stops traveling forward. Objects that block light are called *opaque.* When light meets an opaque surface, it is reflected or absorbed—or a combination of both. (Examples: cardboard, aluminum foil, a brick, wood, metal)
- Objects that let some light pass through them are *translucent,* meaning you can't really see through them, but when you shine a light on them, the light comes through. (Examples: paper towel, tissue paper, waxed paper, lamp shade, clouds)
- Objects that let rays of light pass through them easily are *transparent,* meaning you can see through them. (Examples: clean air, clean water, clear glass, plastic wrap)

Introducing The Lesson:

If it is a sunny day, take students outside and have them observe their shadows. (If the weather does not permit this activity, ask students to recall what their shadows look like and how they occur.) Then tell students that although their bodies cast shadows, not all objects create shadows.

Steps:

1. Share the Background Information about transparent, translucent, and opaque objects on page 205.

2. Show students the three objects you gathered (see the materials list on page 205). For each object ask students to predict if a lot of light, a little light, or no light at all will go through it. Then turn off the lights and darken the room. One at a time, hold each object in front of the flashlight (or up to another light), and have students check their predictions.

3. Distribute page 207 to each student. Provide time for each student to complete the reproducible.

Looking Into Light

Objects that allow a lot of light to pass through them are *transparent.*
Objects that allow some light to pass through them are *translucent.*
Objects that do not let any light pass through them are *opaque.*

Read the words and phrases in the Word Bank below.
Write each word or phrase in the correct column to show how much light
   passes through the item.

Transparent	Translucent	Opaque

Word Bank

waxed paper
paper towel
cardboard
clean water
aluminum foil
clear glass
plastic wrap
tissue paper
wood
black poster board
cloud
clean air

List five other items below.
For each one, write if it is transparent, translucent, or
   opaque.

Example: lamp shade–translucent

1. _____

2. _____

3. _____

4. _____

5. _____

How To Extend The Lesson:

- Use the following experiments to show students how objects can change their *opacity:*
  —Hold an uninflated balloon up to the light and ask students if they can see through it *(no; it appears opaque).* Then ask students to predict whether they would be able to see through the balloon if it were blown up. After taking a class poll, blow up the balloon and have students look at it. Students will be amazed to see that the balloon is now translucent: they can see some light pass through it.
  —Hold one piece of tissue paper to the light and ask students if they can see through it. Then place several sheets of tissue paper atop the first sheet and hold this stack to the light. Students will realize that they cannot see through several layers of tissue paper.

- Reinforce the concept of *shadows* with this bright activity. Set up an overhead projector and gather a variety of small, opaque objects that make interesting shadows, such as a paper clip, scissors, a key, and a bottle of glue. To begin, remind students that some objects block light completely, creating shadows of the objects. Then have students close their eyes as you place one of the objects on the overhead projector. Wrap pieces of tagboard or other suitable material around the projector's tray to block students' view of the object. Project it on the screen. Next have students open their eyes and guess what object is making the shadow on the screen. Allow several guesses before revealing the object. Continue in this manner for each object.

- Invite students to make shadow figures. To do this, set up a projector screen or mount a large sheet of white bulletin-board paper on the wall. Then shine a bright light on the screen. Teach students how to make the shadow figures shown; then encourage them to experiment with the light to create their own shadow figures.

Quacking Duck

Flying Bird

Crocodile

Sound Investigations

Your students will be all ears as they try to identify the sources of different sounds.

Skill: Identifying sources of sounds

Estimated Lesson Time: 30 minutes

Teacher Preparation:
Duplicate page 211 for each student.

Materials:
1 copy of page 211 per student
several sheets of duplicating
    paper
1 large paper grocery bag
scissors
stapler
pencil sharpener
pencil
spiral notebook

Background Information:
Sound is produced by the vibrations of an object. When an object vibrates, the object causes the molecules in the air to start vibrating. The *vibrations* (or *sound waves*) move outward in all directions from the object. These vibrations enter your ears, and your ears convert them to *nerve impulses*. The nerve impulses are then relayed to your brain, where they are interpreted as sounds.

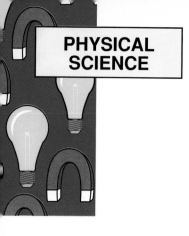

Introducing The Lesson:

Tell your students to close their eyes and listen very carefully. Walk to one side of the classroom and clap your hands together three times. Move back to your original position and ask students to open their eyes. Ask them if they can identify the sound they heard while their eyes were closed. Confirm that the sound was clapping. Then ask students if they can determine where you were standing when you clapped your hands. Confirm the answer by again moving to that side of the classroom and clapping your hands.

Steps:

1. Tell students that although they could not see where you were or what you were doing, their ears were able to provide them with information. Share the Background Information on page 209 to explain how we hear sounds.

2. Distribute a copy of page 211 to each student. Read the directions with students.

   A. To begin, direct students to close their eyes. Crumple a sheet of paper; then hide it in the grocery bag. Ask students to open their eyes and write on the reproducible what they think the sound was.

   B. Repeat this procedure for 2 through 8 on the reproducible. Some sounds you could make include the following:
      - tearing a sheet of paper
      - cutting paper with scissors
      - stapling a sheet of paper
      - dropping a ball of paper on the floor
      - sharpening a pencil
      - tearing paper from a spiral notebook
      - closing a door

3. When you have finished, ask students to share their guesses for each sound; then show them how each sound was made. Have each student record this answer in the second column on his paper.

4. Challenge students to complete the Bonus Box activity.

Name _____

Sound Investigations

Close your eyes and listen carefully to each sound.
At your teacher's signal, open your eyes and write what you
   think you heard.
Then discuss your answers and write what made each sound.

What I Think I Heard	**What Really Made The Sound**
1.	
2.	
3.	
4.	
5.	
6.	
7.	
8.	

Bonus Box: Close your eyes and listen to the sounds in the classroom. Then open your eyes and on the back of this paper, write five different sounds that you heard.

How To Extend The Lesson:

- Repeat the activity using the reproducible on page 211 that is described on page 210, but use a different series of sounds. Or, if desired, ask student volunteers to create sounds for this extension. Have the class again record their impressions and the actual sounds on additional copies of page 211.

- Take your students outside, and have them close their eyes and listen to the different sounds. After three minutes have passed, ask students to open their eyes and identify as many sounds that they heard as they can. Repeat the activity in a variety of settings, such as the cafeteria, the playground, the library, the gymnasium, and the hallway.

- Play a portion of a videotape for your students; then turn off the tape and have them list (on provided paper) the background noises they heard. Rewind the tape, and instruct the students to keep their eyes closed and listen again for background noises in the movie. Next have your students open their eyes and list the different sounds they heard. Ask your students to determine if the noises were as noticeable when they were both watching and listening at the same time as they were when students listened with their eyes closed.

- Have your students create a sound-effects recording on a cassette tape. Challenge them to find a way to simulate thunder, a horse galloping, ocean waves, rain, or the wind blowing. Extend the activity by challenging your students to write a dialogue or play that incorporates the sound effects. If desired, have students perform what they wrote complete with the sound effects.

That's Nurse Linda!

- Share *Science Magic With Sound* by Chris Oxlade (Barron's Educational Series, Inc.; 1994). Students are sure to enjoy trying the entertaining magic tricks that use sound as the trickster. Each trick includes directions for preparing and performing the trick, as well as a scientific explanation.

Good morning, third graders!

- Tape-record voices of teachers and other faculty members. Play this tape for your class and have students try to identify each voice on the tape.

Hot Stuff!

Warm up your students with this red-hot activity for recognizing different sources of heat!

Skill: Identifying sources of heat

Estimated Lesson Time: 30 minutes

Teacher Preparation:
Duplicate page 215 for each student.

Materials:
1 copy of page 215 per student
scissors
glue

Background Information:
There are two main sources of heat: *natural* and *man-made.* Natural sources include sunshine, volcanoes, hot springs, and lightning. Man-made sources include heat caused by friction (striking a match, running a car engine) and heat harnessed from the flow of electrons (almost all electrical appliances). Both sources of heat are important to people, for without harnessed heat, we would not have the convenience of modern appliances. Without natural heat, we would really be in trouble since we depend on the sun to keep our planet warm enough to live on!

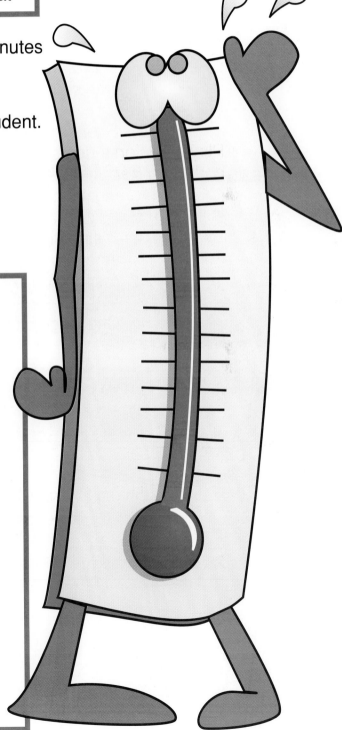

Identifying sources of heat **213**

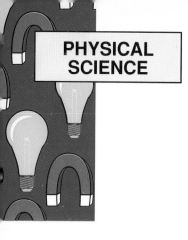

Introducing The Lesson:

Get your class all warmed up for the lesson by having them generate a little heat. Tell your students to place their hands with their palms together and quickly rub them back and forth. Ask students to describe what happens to their hands; then confirm that heat is generated.

Steps:

1. Explain that there are two main sources of heat: *natural* and *man-made.* Ask students to guess which type of heat was created by rubbing their hands together *(man-made).*

2. Share the Background Information on page 213 with your students. Then ask them to brainstorm different sources of heat while you record their answers on the chalkboard as shown.

3. Distribute a copy of page 215 to each student. Instruct students to cut out and glue each source of heat in its corresponding column.

4. Challenge students to complete the Bonus Box activity.

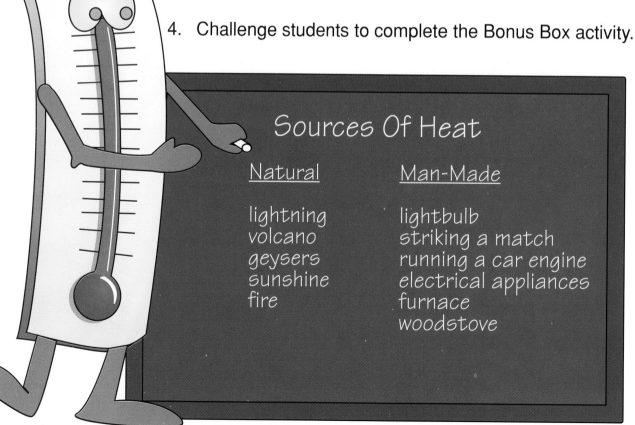

Sources Of Heat

Natural	Man-Made
lightning	lightbulb
volcano	striking a match
geysers	running a car engine
sunshine	electrical appliances
fire	furnace
	woodstove

Hot Stuff!

Heat can come from a *natural source,* such as a forest fire.
It can also come from a *man-made source,* such as a microwave.

Cut out each heat source below.
Glue each picture in the correct column.

Bonus Box: On the back of this sheet, list the different sources of heat you have used today.

Natural	Man-Made

©The Education Center, Inc. • *Ready-to-Go Lessons* • TEC1116 Key p. 319

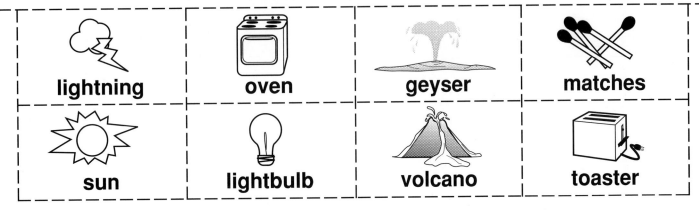

lightning   oven   geyser   matches

sun   lightbulb   volcano   toaster

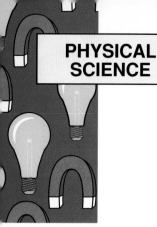

How To Extend The Lesson:

- Challenge students to think about the many sources of heat they use each day. Assign each student a room of a house and have him list the different sources of heat often found in that room. Enlist students' help in compiling the findings onto a chart labeled "Heat In Our Homes."

- Show students what a powerful source of heat the sun is. Place each of two ice cubes in a separate, clear plastic cup. Leave one cup in the classroom and place the other outside in direct sunlight. Have students observe the two cups to see the difference in melting time.

- Divide students in pairs, and instruct each pair to name and write ten things that are associated with heat. Challenge each pair to use the words to create a word-search puzzle. Then have each twosome trade puzzles with another pair and find the words on that list.

- Have each student cut out pictures of heat sources from discarded magazines. Collect the pictures and place them in a decorated container. Duplicate a class supply of the heat-source cards below. Give each student one of each card. Have the student color his cards and glue them back-to-back with a craft stick between them. Then randomly draw a picture of a heat source from the container and show it to the class. Each student holds his craft stick so that the appropriate card is facing you. Continue in this manner until all the pictures have been drawn.

Patterns

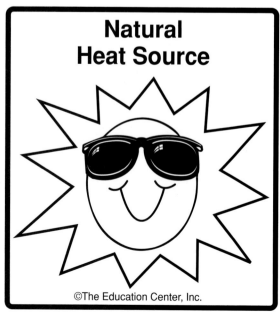

Natural Heat Source

©The Education Center, Inc.

Man-Made Heat Source

©The Education Center, Inc.

©The Education Center, Inc. • *Ready-to-Go Lessons* • TEC1116

Cosmic Order

Launch into this solar-system game that will help teach your students the order of the planets.

Skill: Learning the order of the planets in our solar system

Estimated Lesson Time: 30 minutes

Teacher Preparation:
1. Duplicate page 219 onto tagboard for each student pair.
2. Write the name of each planet on a separate sheet of 12" x 18" construction paper.

Materials:
1 tagboard copy of page 219 per student pair
9 labeled sheets of construction paper
1 pair of scissors per student pair

Background Information:
- The first four planets (known as the *inner planets*) are made of rock. The remaining five planets (the *outer planets*) are composed mainly of gases.
- The order of the planets from the sun is the following:
  Mercury, Venus, Earth, Mars, Jupiter, Saturn, Uranus, Neptune, Pluto.
- Refer to the chart at the right to find each planet's distance from the sun.

Planets	Average Distance From The Sun (in millions of miles)
Pluto	3,688
Neptune	2,794
Uranus	1,784
Saturn	887
Jupiter	483
Mars	142
Earth	93
Venus	67
Mercury	36

Sun

Introducing The Lesson:

Randomly distribute the nine labeled sheets of construction paper to different student volunteers. Tell the class that these students are going to represent planets. Have each student hold the sign so that the labeled side can be read by her classmates. Then explain to the class that they are going to learn the order of the planets.

Steps:

1. Designate an object in the classroom to be the sun. Then, as you share the Background Information on page 217, position each volunteer side by side in her corresponding order from the sun.

2. Ask the student closest to the sun to announce her planet's name. Then have the next student in line announce the name of his planet, and so on, until all nine planet names have been announced. Collect and redistribute the planet signs to additional volunteers. Challenge these students to sequence themselves. If desired, ask the remaining students to provide assistance as needed.

3. Then, to reinforce this information, have students play the card game Cosmic Concentration. Pair students and give each twosome a tagboard copy of page 219 and a pair of scissors. Have one student from each pair cut apart the planet cards.

4. Instruct students to play the game as follows:

   • Spread out the cards and turn them facedown on the playing surface.
   • Students take turns turning over a card to find Mercury, the first planet from the sun.
   • The student who finds Mercury first keeps that card and takes another turn, this time looking for Venus (the second planet from the sun).
   • Play continues in this same manner as students take turns looking for the planet that comes next in the order. When a student finds a correct card, she adds it to her stack and takes another turn.
   • The student with the most cards at the end of the game is the winner.

Cosmic Concentration
For Two Players

1. Cut out the game cards.
2. Spread out the cards and place them facedown.
3. Follow your teacher's directions to play the game.

Mercury	Venus	Earth
closest planet to the sun	second planet from the sun	third planet from the sun
Mars	**Jupiter**	**Saturn**
fourth planet from the sun	fifth planet from the sun	sixth planet from the sun
Uranus	**Neptune**	**Pluto**
seventh planet from the sun	eighth planet from the sun	ninth planet from the sun

How To Extend The Lesson:

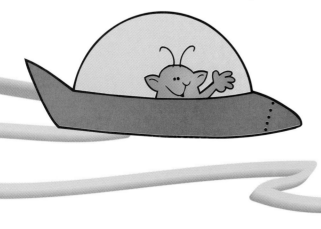

- Display the sentence "**M**y **V**ery **E**ducated **M**other **J**ust **S**erved **U**s **N**ine **P**ickles." Show students that the first letter of each word corresponds with the first letter of each planet in the solar system and that they are arranged in the planets' correct order from the sun. Challenge students to create other silly sentences to help them recall the planets in order.

- Read aloud *The Magic School Bus® Lost In The Solar System* by Joanna Cole (Scholastic Inc., 1992). Have each student write a version of this story in which your class becomes lost in the solar system and has an astronomical adventure.

- Share some out-of-this-world poetry with your students. *Blast Off!: Poems About Space* selected by Lee Bennett Hopkins (HarperCollins Children's Books, 1995) is a collection of poems about the planets, astronauts, and mysteries of space. After reading the poetry aloud, encourage your class to compose poems that celebrate space.

- Demonstrate to students the revolutions of the planets with this nifty idea. You will need the planet signs from the introduction to this lesson and an additional sign labeled "Sun." Distribute a sign to each of ten students. Position the student holding the sign labeled "Sun" in the center of an open area; then place the planets in their correct order. Have the planet students walk around the Sun in a circle at the same pace. After revolving around the Sun once, ask students which planet took the shortest amount of time. Which planet took the longest amount of time? Why?

The Planetary Times

Send your students into orbit with this far-out writing assignment!

Skill: Researching planets

Estimated Lesson Time: 45 minutes

Teacher Preparation:

1. Duplicate page 223 for each student.
2. Gather reference materials about the planets that are suitable for your students' reading levels.
3. If desired, post a copy of the Background Information shown below and make a transparency of the diagram on page 222.

Materials:

1 copy of page 223 per student
reference materials with planet information
overhead projector and transparency (optional)

Background Information:

Share the following planetary data with your students:

Planet	Length of day (in Earth time)	Length of year (in Earth time)	Moons	Rings
Mercury	59 days	88 days	0	0
Venus	243 days	225 days	0	0
Earth	24 hours	365 days	1	0
Mars	25 hours	687 days	2	0
Jupiter	10 hours	12 years	16 or more	yes
Saturn	11 hours	30 years	17 or more	yes
Uranus	17 hours	84 years	15 or more	yes
Neptune	16 hours	165 years	8	yes
Pluto	6 days	248 years	1	0

Introducing The Lesson:

Inform students that they will review our solar system in a headline-making way. Ask each student to imagine that she is an interplanetary news reporter. Her assignment is to report the facts, interesting details, and newsworthy data of her assigned planet.

Steps:

1. Assign each student a planet to research. Provide reference materials and, if desired, display a copy of the Background Information on page 221 and a transparency of the diagram shown below.

2. Distribute a copy of page 223 to each student. Provide time for students to research their planets and complete the reproducible.

3. Encourage students to compose catchy headlines for the Our Feature Story section.

4. Provide time for students to share their papers with your class. Then post the completed papers on a bulletin board covered with discarded newspapers.

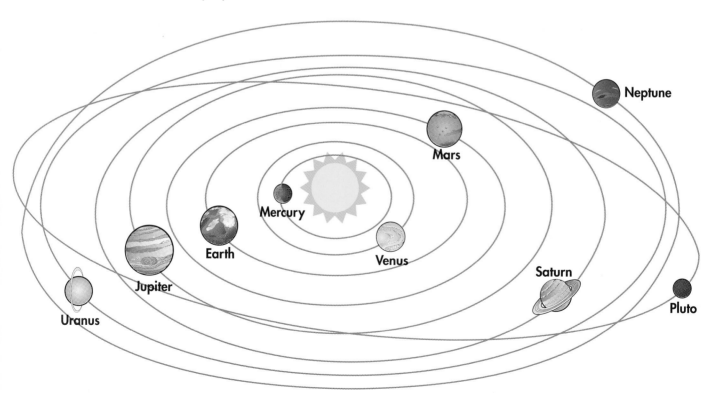

THE PLANETARY TIMES

Issue Published by _____ Date _____

WEATHER REPORT (temperature)

OUR FEATURE STORY

_____
(planet name)

This planet looks like:

LOCATION (distance from the sun)

MOONS • RINGS • DIAMETER • GRAVITY • DESCRIPTION • LENGTH OF A DAY • WHEN DISCOVERED

FASCINATING FACTS

1. _____

2. _____

3. _____

4. _____

5. _____

How To Extend The Lesson:

- Integrate creative writing and science by extending the newspaper theme. To do this, challenge each student to create a second page for his newspaper that features a planet-related comic strip, an advice column, advertisements, and want ads. Remind students to use their imaginations—the sky's the limit!

- Challenge your class to use their knowledge of the planets in a guessing game. Have each student write five clues about the planet of his choice on a slip of paper. Then ask each student, in turn, to read his clues to the class. After the clues have been given, have the reader call on a volunteer to identify the planet. If the volunteer answers correctly, he may read his clues to the class. If the volunteer answers incorrectly, have the student call on additional classmates until the correct planet is given. Play continues in the same manner until all students have read their clues.

- Have your students take a comparative look at the planets with a diagraming activity. To do this, pair students, and have each twosome complete a Venn diagram showing how two planets are alike and different. For an added challenge, instruct the partners to compose a report of their findings. Display the completed diagrams on a bulletin board titled "Pairing Up The Planets."

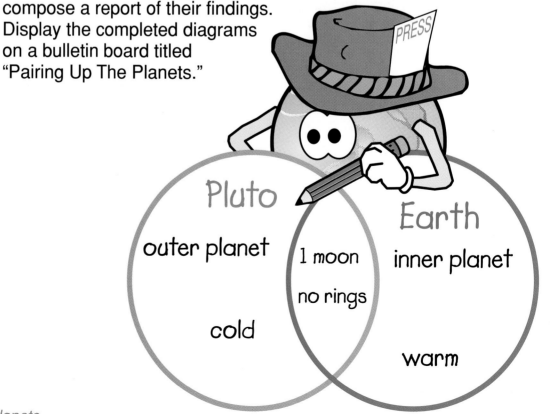

Habitat Hunt

From mountains to valleys, and from jungles to deserts, students will explore the characteristics that make each habitat a special place.

Skill: Researching Earth's habitats

Estimated Lesson Time: 45 minutes

Teacher Preparation:
1. Duplicate page 227 for each student.
2. Gather appropriate reference materials for a variety of Earth's habitats.

Materials:
1 copy of page 227 per student
reference materials
crayons

Background Information:
A habitat is a place where plants and animals live. Different habitats include deserts, temperate forests, grasslands, oceans, tropical rain forests, polar regions, and mountains.

Introducing The Lesson:

Tell your students that you are thinking of getting a new pet. You have it narrowed down to two choices—a goldfish and an elephant. Ask students to help you consider which pet would feel more at home with you.

Steps:

1. Record responses on the chalkboard as students consider the environmental needs of each pet. Then ask students to explain why a goldfish would make a better pet for you.

2. Share the Background Information on page 225. Explain that each habitat has special features that make it different from the others, such as the climate, the landforms, and the types of plant and animal life.

3. Distribute a copy of page 227 to each student. Divide students into seven small groups and assign each group a habitat to research. Have each group share the appropriate research materials to complete the reproducible.

4. Challenge students to complete the Bonus Box activity.

Name _____

Habitat Hunt

Use an encyclopedia or a reference book to find out information about your assigned habitat.

Habitat name: _____

The temperature ranges from _____ to _____.

The weather is usually _____ in the summer and _____ in the winter.

Some animals that live in this habitat:

1. _____
2. _____
3. _____
4. _____
5. _____

Draw the habitat.

The habitat looks like this:

Some plants that live in this habitat:

1. _____
2. _____
3. _____
4. _____
5. _____

Some special things about this habitat:

1. _____
   _____.
2. _____
   _____.
3. _____
   _____.

Bonus Box: Draw a picture of the habitat on the back of this paper.

How To Extend The Lesson:

• Ask each group to share information about its habitat with the class. After each group has shared, challenge students to compare and contrast the different habitats. Then have students decide which type of habitat best describes their living area.

• Assist each group in finding its habitat on a world map.

• Have each group create a poster or mural showing the landforms, plants, and animals of its assigned habitat. Post the completed projects on a classroom wall; then invite other classes to visit your classroom for a habitat tour.

• Encourage creative-writing skills by having each student design a travel brochure for one of Earth's habitats. Demonstrate how to fold a sheet of drawing paper into thirds to create a brochure format. Have students do the same. Instruct each student to write facts about her chosen habitat on the brochure as well as possible entertainment options and travel accommodations. Encourage students to share their completed brochures with their classmates.

• Reward students for their hard work with personalized copies of the award below.

Congratulations, _____ for your hard work with habitats!

Journey To The Center Of Earth

Your students will dig this game that reviews information about Earth's layers!

Skill: Reviewing Earth's layers

Estimated Lesson Time: 30 minutes

Teacher Preparation:
1. Duplicate page 231 for each student pair.
2. Display the Background Information below on an overhead projector, on chart paper, or on the chalkboard.

Materials:
1 copy of page 231 per student pair
display of Background Information
1 die per student pair
1 game marker per student
1 peanut M&M's® per student

Background Information:
- Earth consists of three basic layers: the crust, mantle, and core.
- The crust is the outermost layer. Its thickness varies from about five miles under the oceans to about 25 miles under the continents.
- The middle layer is called the mantle. It is made of rock and is about 1,800 miles thick.
- The innermost layer is the core. There are two sections of the core. The outer core is believed to be liquid. The inner core is believed to be solid.
- The total distance from the crust to the center of the earth is about 4,000 miles.

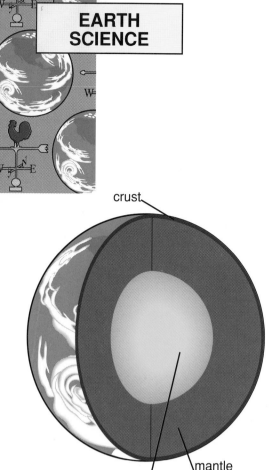

crust

mantle

core

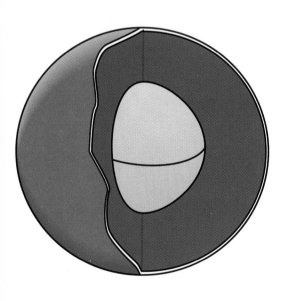

Introducing The Lesson:

Distribute a peanut M&M's® to each student. Instruct the students to carefully bite their candies in half and examine the cross section. Ask students to describe what they see. Explain that the three layers of the candy are similar to the three layers of Earth. The candy shell represents the crust, the chocolate represents the mantle, and the peanut represents the core.

Steps:

1. Invite students to eat their candies as you discuss the Background Information on page 229. Inform students that they will refer to this information as they play a game that reviews facts about Earth's layers.

2. Pair students and distribute a die, two game markers, and a copy of page 231 to each student pair.

3. Explain the rules for the game as follows:
   • Each player rolls the die to determine who will go first. The player with the higher roll takes the first turn.
   • The first player places his game marker on Start and rolls the die. He moves his marker the determined number of spaces.
   • If the player lands on a space with a question and answers it correctly, he stays at that space. (Leave the Background Information on display for the students to refer to.) If he answers incorrectly, he must return to his previous space on the gameboard. If he lands on a space with instructions, he follows the instructions. Either way, his turn ends.
   • The first player to reach the inner core with an exact roll is the winner.

4. If time allows, have students change partners and play the game again.

Journey To The Center Of Earth

Place your game pieces on Start.
Roll the die and move ahead that many spaces.
Follow the directions or answer the question in each space.
The first player to reach the inner core by exact roll is the
    winner!

How To Extend The Lesson:

• Provide each student with three small balls of clay in different colors. Instruct the students to construct a model of Earth using a different color for each layer. Then provide each student with a plastic knife to cut the model in half so that a cross section of the layers is shown.

• Have a local meteorologist or scientist visit your classroom to explain how earthquakes and volcanic eruptions occur.

• Make a copy of page 231, and reprogram it with a new set of questions about Earth's layers. If desired, have your students brainstorm a list of questions to use in reprogramming the game.

• Read to your class *The Magic School Bus® Inside The Earth* by Joanna Cole (Scholastic Inc., 1989). After sharing the story, provide materials for your students to make posters showing the inside of Earth. Challenge your students to label the depths and temperatures of each layer.

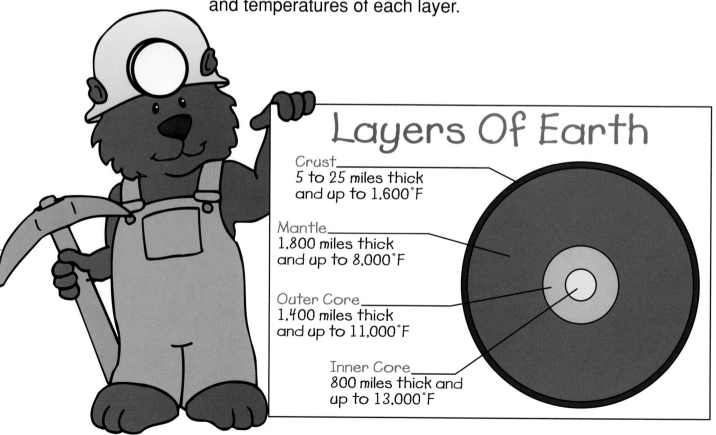

Layers Of Earth

Crust
5 to 25 miles thick
and up to 1,600°F

Mantle
1,800 miles thick
and up to 8,000°F

Outer Core
1,400 miles thick
and up to 11,000°F

Inner Core
800 miles thick and
up to 13,000°F

Rock Detectives

Dig into a study of rocks with this gem of a classification activity!

Skill: Investigating rocks

Estimated Lesson Time: 45 minutes

Teacher Preparation:

1. Duplicate page 235 for each student.
2. Have students go outside and gather (or gather in advance) two different-type rocks apiece. Or provide each student with two rocks.
3. For each student cut two 2-inch construction-paper squares: one from black paper and one from white paper.
4. Set up an area in the classroom where students have access to a bottle of vinegar and an eyedropper.

Materials:

1 copy of page 235 per student
1 eyedropper
1 bottle of vinegar
2 rocks of assorted types per student
2 distinctly different rocks for teacher demonstration
1 paper clip per student
1 penny per student
1 two-inch square each of black paper and white paper

Background Information:

- Geologists measure the hardness of minerals in rocks from 1 (soft) to 10 (hard). Talc has a rating of 1 and can be scratched by a fingernail. Calcite has a rating of 3 and can be scratched by a penny. A diamond has a rating of 10 and can be scratched only by another diamond. The hardness rating of some common materials: fingernail—2.5; copper penny—3.0; and steel knife—5.5–6.5.
- If vinegar bubbles when placed on a rock, calcium carbonate is present in the rock. Rocks such as limestone and marble will cause vinegar to fizz because they contain calcium carbonate.

Introducing The Lesson:

Tell students that they are going to be *rock hounds* for the following lesson. Ask students to guess what a *rock hound* is. Then explain that the term is used to describe someone who collects or studies rocks.

Steps:

1. Share the Background Information on page 233 with your students. Explain that in addition to the hardness of rocks, geologists also look at color, texture, shape, and other attributes.

2. Show students the two rocks you gathered. Pass the rocks around and ask students to observe similarities and differences in the rocks. Tell students that scientists use similarities and differences to classify rocks.

3. Distribute a copy of page 235, a paper clip, and a penny to each student. Also provide students with access to the eyedropper and the vinegar. Have students place the rocks they gathered (or you gave them) on their desks. Review the directions; then have each student complete the reproducible.

4. Challenge students to complete the Bonus Box activity.

sniff, sniff

Name _____

Rock Detectives

Name your rocks "Rock One" and "Rock Two."
Follow the directions to observe and experiment
with your rocks.

	Rock One	Rock Two
1. Describe the color of each rock.		
2. Describe the size and the shape of each rock.		
3. Describe the way each rock feels.		
4. Scratch each rock with your fingernail, a penny, and a paper clip. List the objects that scratch each rock's surface.		
5. What happens when you rub each rock across: the black paper?		
the white paper?		
6. What happens when you put a few drops of vinegar on each rock?		

7. Complete the following statements:

My rocks are alike because _____

_____

My rocks are different because _____

_____

Bonus Box: Choose one rock. Write a story from its point of view.

How To Extend The Lesson:

- Have students find the length and mass of their rocks. Provide a scale and measuring tape for students to use individually or in pairs.

- Share *Sylvester And The Magic Pebble* by William Steig (Simon & Schuster Books For Young Readers, 1988). Have each student write a story telling what could happen if one of her rocks had magical powers.

- This activity encourages students to explore the benefits of pet rocks. To begin have each student make a pet rock. To do this, a student uses craft glue to attach wiggle eyes to a rock. Next he uses paint pens to draw facial features. Then he adds yarn lengths for hair. After creating and naming his pet rock, have each student create a small poster encouraging others to create pet rocks. Ask students to list several positive benefits of having a pet rock compared with a dog or a cat.

- Have students bring rocks from home. Set up a center with a magnifying glass and a reference book of rocks and minerals. Encourage students to research their rocks.

- Duplicate and personalize copies of the award below for students.

Award

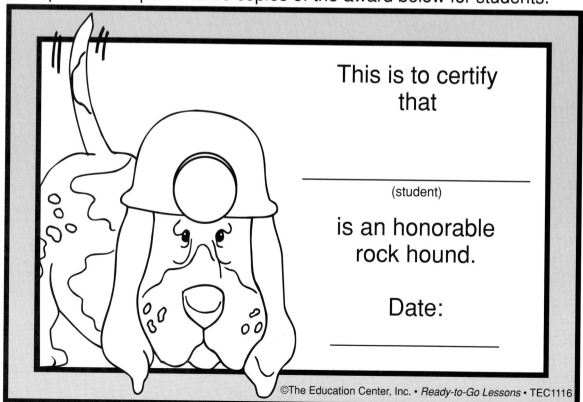

This is to certify that

_____
(student)

is an honorable rock hound.

Date:

_____

Our Changing Earth

Explore the changes to Earth's surface with a hands-on lesson about water and soil erosion.

Skill: Recognizing the signs of erosion

Estimated Lesson Time: 45 minutes

Teacher Preparation:
Duplicate a copy of page 239 for each student.

Materials:
1 copy of page 239 per student
1 clipboard or other portable writing surface per
  student
1 drinking straw per student
1 large, shallow box lid
dry sand
gravel
1 eyedropper
water

Background Information:
Earth's surface can be changed in many ways. Natural forces—such as ice, wind, and water—continuously wear away, break down, and erode Earth's surface. Ice can form in the cracks of rocks and break them apart. Waves can wear down cliffs. Streams and rivers break off rocks and carry them away. Wind can wear down rocks and move sand and soil to new areas. Because of these continuous forces, Earth's surface is in a constant state of change.

Introducing The Lesson:

Tell students that while they were sleeping last night, there were many changes on Earth. Explain that every time the wind blows, every time a wave hits a beach, and every time the ground freezes, there are changes to Earth.

Steps:

1. Share the Background Information on page 237 with your students. Then tell students that they are going to experiment to see how these forces change Earth.

2. Place enough sand in the box lid to form a small hill. Distribute a straw to each student. Provide the opportunity for each student to blow through the straw at the hill of sand and observe the effects of "wind" on soil.

3. Rebuild the hill; then have the students take turns filling the eyedropper with water and squirting it in the sand to observe the effects of water on soil.

4. Repeat the experiment using gravel instead of sand. Ask students which surface is more easily affected by wind and water.

5. Distribute a copy of page 239 and a portable writing surface to each student. Review the directions; then have students complete the reproducible as you take them on a walk around the school grounds to look for signs of erosion.

6. Back in the classroom, have students share their findings.

7. Challenge students to complete the Bonus Box activity.

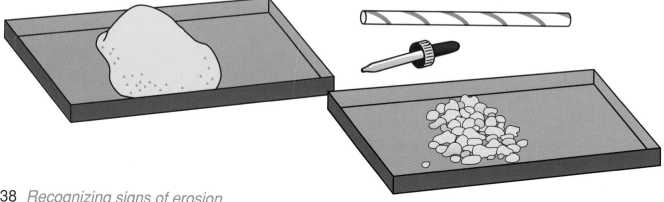

Our Changing Earth

Earth is always changing.
Wind, ice, and water can break up rocks
   and move soil.
When rocks and soil are moved by natural
   forces, we call it **erosion.**

Look outside for signs of erosion.
Use the checklist as you look.
Write down any other findings.

	Observed	Possible Cause
Cracks in the sidewalk	yes ☐ no ☐	
Areas of soil washed away	yes ☐ no ☐	
Smooth, rounded rocks	yes ☐ no ☐	
Water collected in a puddle	yes ☐ no ☐	
Signs or statues that are worn	yes ☐ no ☐	
Paint worn away	yes ☐ no ☐	
Soil drifts against a building	yes ☐ no ☐	
Cracks in the ground	yes ☐ no ☐	
Other: _____ _____	yes ☐ no ☐	

Bonus Box: On the back of this sheet, List some areas around your house where you might find signs of erosion.

How To Extend The Lesson:

- Have your students experiment to see which surfaces are more resistant to water erosion. Have each student fill an eyedropper with water and observe the absorption on a variety of surfaces. Encourage them to observe drops of water on a desktop, a paper towel, potting soil, an aluminum plate, construction paper, a sponge, cardboard, a plastic ruler, and a wooden ruler.

- Have each student write a narrative describing something he left outside that was changed by natural forces. Encourage students to illustrate their stories with before and after pictures.

- Introduce your students to national parks that show signs of nature's forces. Some examples include:
  —Yosemite Valley (California): glacier erosion
  —Grand Canyon (Arizona): water erosion
  —Mammoth Cave National Park (Kentucky): mildly acidic water

- Encourage your students to look for newspaper articles or pictures about how wind or water has changed Earth. Discuss whether each change was a positive or negative one. Post the pictures and articles on a current-events bulletin board.

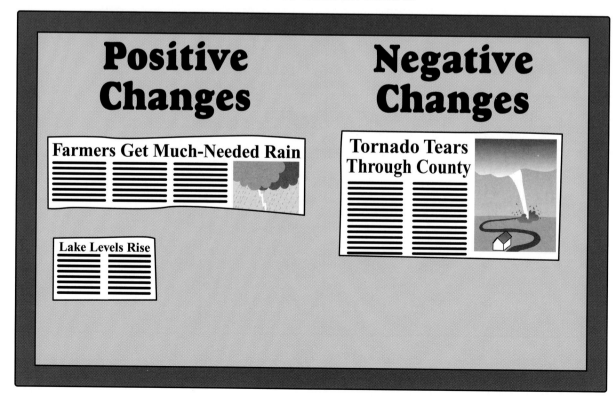

Targeting Communities

Strengthen your sharpshooters' understanding of community settings with this motivating lesson!

Skill: Identifying urban, suburban, and rural settings

Estimated Lesson Time: 30 minutes

Teacher Preparation:

1. Duplicate page 243 for each student.
2. Draw a large target on the chalkboard. Starting from the center, label each section from the center out "urban," "suburban," and "rural" (see the illustration below).

Materials:

1 copy of page 243 for each student
scissors
glue
crayons

Background Information:

There are three major community settings. An *urban* setting is in the city. A *suburban* setting has to do with a community that is just outside of or close to a city. A *rural* setting has to do with the country.

Although each of the community settings have features in common, such as homes, they also have differences. For example, a skyscraper might be found in the city but probably not in the country.

Introducing The Lesson:

Ask students to think about the area in which they live. Encourage students to discuss the characteristics of their community, such as parks, schools, and trees. Next ask students if everyone lives in the same type of community as they do. Confirm that people live in different types of communities; then share the Background Information on page 241.

Steps:

1. Direct students' attention to the target on the chalkboard. Tell students to name characteristics that describe an urban setting. Write their responses in the corresponding section of the target (see the example below). Repeat this step for suburban and rural.

2. Distribute a copy of page 243 to each student. Review the directions with students and have each child complete the page independently.

3. Challenge students to complete the Bonus Box activity.

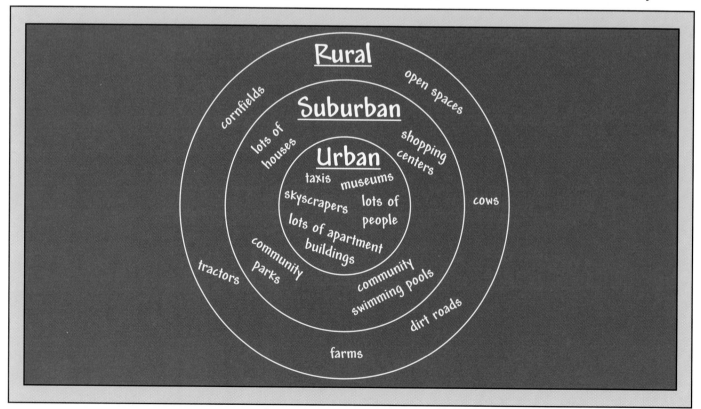

Name _____

Targeting Communities

Write a definition for each community setting. Then read each card at the bottom of the page.
Decide which cards best fit in each community. Next color and cut out each card. Glue each card on its matching tree.

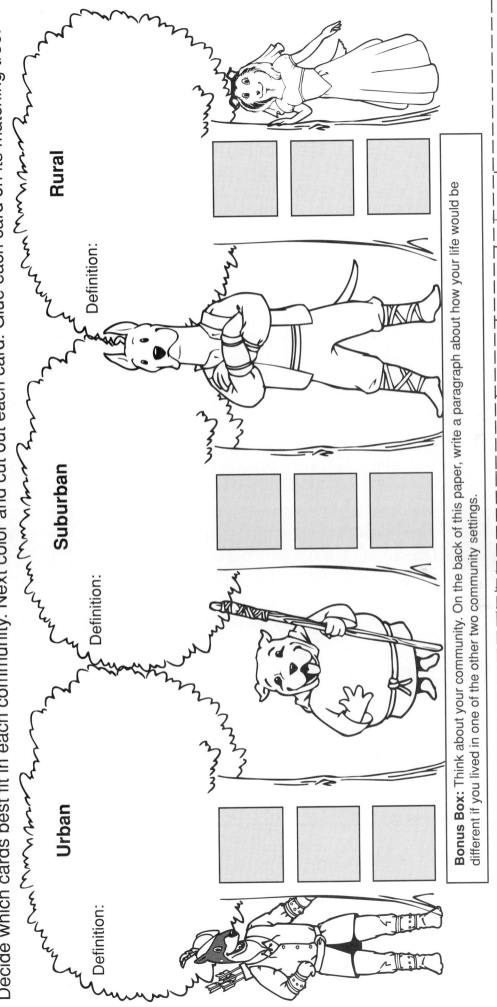

Rural

Definition:

Suburban

Definition:

Urban

Definition:

Bonus Box: Think about your community. On the back of this paper, write a paragraph about how your life would be different if you lived in one of the other two community settings.

community parks

museums

cows

tractors

houses

cornfields

skyscrapers

community swimming pools

taxis

How To Extend The Lesson:

- Youngsters take aim at community settings with this center idea. First make a set of flash cards. On the front of each card, write a characteristic of one of the three community settings. On the back, write the setting to which the characteristic belongs. Then make a large target, labeling each section with a point value. Place the flash cards, the target, a beanbag, a supply of paper, and a pencil at the center. To complete the activity, a student places the target on the floor. Then he reads the front of a flash card, decides what the setting is, and checks his answer. If he is correct, he tosses the beanbag on the target and writes down the number of points he earned. If he is incorrect, he places the card in a discard pile and reviews it at the end of the game. He continues in this manner until all cards have been reviewed; then he totals his points and tries to beat that score the next time he plays.

- Showcase a collection of student work with this bulletin board idea. Give each student a white paper plate and a copy of the pattern below. In the center of the paper plate, instruct the student to color a picture of one of the three community settings. Then have her color the outer ridge of the plate red. On the arrow, direct her to write three descriptive sentences about the setting she drew. Then have her cut out the arrow, flip it over, and write the setting near the tip. Mount each paper plate and arrow (as shown) on a bulletin board titled "Hit The Bull's-Eye!" Encourage students to read the descriptions and then lift the tip of the arrow to check their guesses.

Pattern

Guess Which Community I Am!

1. _____

2. _____

3. _____

©The Education Center, Inc. • *Ready-to-Go Lessons* • TEC1116

Helping Hands

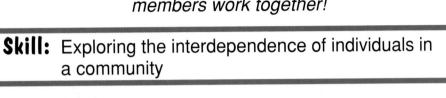

Help students learn that everyone wins when community members work together!

Skill: Exploring the interdependence of individuals in a community

Estimated Lesson Time: 45 minutes

Teacher Preparation:

1. Duplicate page 247 for each student.
2. Using a 12" x 18" sheet of construction paper, scissors, and markers, make a class puzzle. To do this, draw a desired picture or design that fills the page. Then cut it into puzzle pieces so that there is one piece for each student.

Materials:

1 copy of page 247 for each student
construction paper
markers
tape
scissors

Background Information:

A *community* is a place where people live and help each other. People in a community help one another by giving money to those in need and by sharing work. For example, doctors, nurses, technicians, and paramedics work together to help people become well. Depending upon one another is called *interdependence*.

Introducing The Lesson:

Give each student a puzzle piece. Explain to students that they will help each other solve a puzzle. In turn, have each student bring her piece to the chalkboard. Encourage the class to work together to determine where the pieces fit and then lightly tape them into place. When the puzzle is completed, acknowledge how the group worked together to finish the task.

Steps:

1. Explain to the class that they will be learning how people in a community work together to help one another. Share the Background Information on page 245.

2. Write the word *firefighter* on the chalkboard. Then ask students how firefighters help the community and list their responses under the word *firefighter*.

3. Repeat Step 2 using the words *police officer* and *emergency medical technician (EMT)*.

4. Distribute a copy of page 247 to each student. Encourage a class discussion about the illustration at the top of page 247. Guide students to understand the role of each person, such as the police officer directs traffic and keeps people out of harm's way. Then have each student complete the page independently.

5. Challenge students to complete the Bonus Box activity.

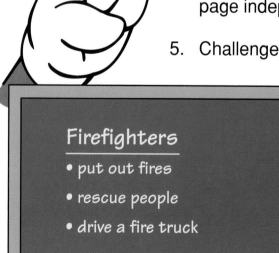

Firefighters

- put out fires
- rescue people
- drive a fire truck

Name _____

Helping Hands

Read each question below.
Use the picture above to answer each question.

1. How does the police officer help the citizens? _____

   _____

2. How does the police officer help the firefighters? _____

   _____

3. How do the EMTs help the firefighters? _____

   _____

4. How does the police officer help the EMTs? _____

   _____

5. How do the firefighters help the EMTs? _____

   _____

Bonus Box: On the back of this paper, write one way the citizens in the picture can help either the firefighters, the police officer, or the EMTs.

How To Extend The Lesson:

- Have students give gifts to their community. On an index card, have each student write one way people in his community could help one another. Then instruct the student to glue his index card to a slightly larger piece of wrapping paper and add a bow. Mount the gifts on a bulletin board entitled "Presents To Our Community!"

- Explain to students that lending a hand at home can be a way of helping the community. Then read *The Berenstain Bears Lend A Helping Hand* by Jan and Stan Berenstain (Random House, Inc.; 1998) to your class. Encourage discussion about how the yard sale provided an opportunity for the cubs and Miz McGrizz to help one another. Next have each student trace her hand on a sheet of construction paper and cut it out. Then, on each finger, have her write a way she helps at home. In the palm, have each student draw a picture of helping at home and write "[Student's Name] Helps Out!" Next use the handprints to make a bulletin-board border or display them on a wall.

- Encourage students to help their community. Choose a day for students to pick up trash from the school grounds or contribute canned goods to needy families. Then reward your community helpers with a copy of the ribbon pattern shown.

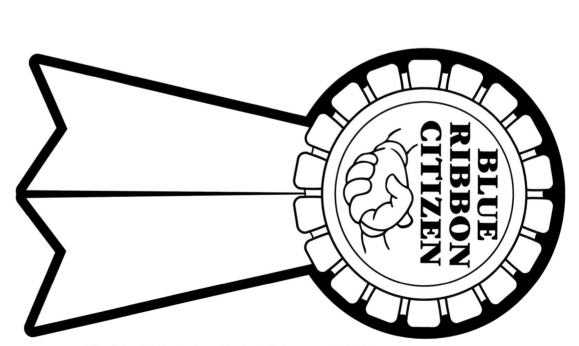

Resource Roundup

Saddle up and get set to teach how natural resources affect community life with this rootin'-tootin' lesson!

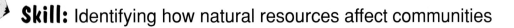

Skill: Identifying how natural resources affect communities

Estimated Lesson Time: 40 minutes

Teacher Preparation:
Duplicate page 251 for each student.

Materials:
1 copy of page 251 for each student

Background Information:
Natural resources are things found in nature that people can use. Natural resources are not made by people. Land, minerals, water, plants, animals, and climate are all natural resources. People use natural resources to make goods, such as food, fuel, and raw materials. Natural resources affect the types of recreation and jobs found in a community.

Introducing The Lesson:

Explain to students that *climate* is the average weather of a place over a period of years. Ask students to describe your community's climate. Record their responses on the chalkboard.

Steps:

1. Share with students the Background Information on page 249. Then ask them to describe how your community is affected by its climate.

2. Have students share examples of other natural resources in your community, such as a river or an ocean. Then ask them to describe how these resources affect the types of recreation (swimming) and jobs (lifeguarding) in your community.

3. Have students brainstorm a list of natural resources found in other communities that are different from theirs (see the list below for suggestions). Write students' ideas on the chalkboard. Challenge them to think of how each resource might affect a community.

4. Distribute a copy of page 251 to each student. Have a volunteer read aloud the directions at the top of the page. Have each child complete the reproducible independently.

Resources In Other Communities

oil	cacti
warm climate	tropical birds
beaches	rainfall
snow	gold
canyons	seafood

Resource Roundup

Read each community's description.
Then read each clue.
Write an "I" next to each clue that describes Iceville.
Write an "S" next to each clue that describes Sunland.

Iceville

Iceville is a community located just below the North Pole. Its growing season is very short. Iceville has a large supply of oil beneath its icy ground. Iceville is located near a large frozen lake. There are also rich mineral deposits in this area.

Sunland

Sunland is a community that has a very warm climate. Sunland has lots of beaches and is a popular vacation spot. The waters near Sunland are full of tuna and other sea life. Sunland's growing season is very long.

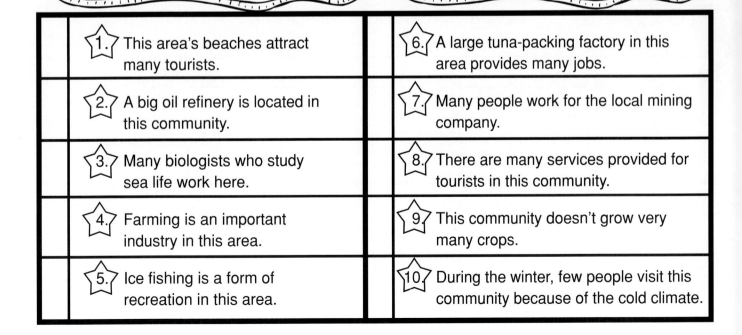

1. This area's beaches attract many tourists.		6. A large tuna-packing factory in this area provides many jobs.
2. A big oil refinery is located in this community.		7. Many people work for the local mining company.
3. Many biologists who study sea life work here.		8. There are many services provided for tourists in this community.
4. Farming is an important industry in this area.		9. This community doesn't grow very many crops.
5. Ice fishing is a form of recreation in this area.		10. During the winter, few people visit this community because of the cold climate.

How To Extend The Lesson:

• This hands-on activity focuses on the natural resources in your community. From discarded magazines, have each child cut out pictures representing natural resources found in your community. Direct him to glue his cutouts on a sheet of construction paper in an overlapping fashion to create a collage. Post the completed projects on a bulletin board titled "Rounding Up Our Natural Resources."

• Divide your class into small groups. Give each group a section of employment ads from your local newspaper. Then have the group cut out three job ads that are based on the natural resources in your community. (These might include an ad for a coal miner, a lifeguard, an oil refinery worker, or a commercial fisherman.) When the allotted time is over, ask each group to name the jobs they found and tell how they relate to your community's natural resources. Discuss with students how the types of jobs might change if your community had different natural resources.

• Have students create brochures featuring the natural resources in your community. With students, brainstorm and write on the chalkboard a list of your community's natural resources. To create a brochure, a student folds a 9" x 12" sheet of white construction paper in thirds. She then unfolds the paper and writes the title "[Community's name]'s Natural Resources" on the back of the first section. Then she personalizes the resulting cover as desired. On each of the five remaining brochure pages, the student writes a sentence about a different resource from the list on the board and illustrates it. After students share their brochures, display the completed projects in your school's media center.

Gators Guard Community Rights

Teach students about community law with this snappy activity!

Skill: Identifying the need for and the use of community laws

Estimated Lesson Time: 45 minutes

Teacher Preparation:
1. Duplicate page 255 for each student.
2. Obtain three or four products with safety labels or cautions, such as a bottle of correction fluid, the package of a toy, and a bottle of glue.

Materials:
1 copy of page 255
3 or 4 products with safety labels or cautions
scissors
glue

Background Information:
Community laws help people live together in a fair way. City leaders decide on laws that will benefit the community and protect the people. Not all communities have the same laws.

Some laws protect the health and safety of people. For example, a law that requires a person to ride his or her bike on the road rather than on the sidewalk protects pedestrians.

Other laws are made to keep order and protect property. For example, dogs that are allowed to roam neighborhoods can destroy property by turning over trash cans and digging in yards. A law that keeps dogs from roaming protects people's property.

Communities are responsible for enforcing the laws. Police officers, judges, and other officials make sure that laws are followed and people who violate them are punished.

Introducing The Lesson:

Display the products that contain safety labels. Ask students why some products come with a safety label. Guide students in understanding that labels protect people by advising them of possible dangers.

Steps:

1. Tell students that, like safety labels on products, community laws help protect people and keep them safe. Next share the Background Information on page 253 with youngsters. Ask students to tell about community laws with which they are familiar. Then lead students in a discussion about why each law listed below is needed. Write their responses on the chalkboard.
   - Do not let your dog roam the community.
   - Remove all poison ivy and poison oak from your yard.
   - Ride your bicycle on the right-hand side of the road.
   - Bag yard clippings rather than burn them.
   - Do not have open barrels or containers in your yard. *(Mosquitoes cause health problems when they breed in the rainwater that collects.)*

2. Distribute a copy of page 255 to each student. Ask a student volunteer to read **Gators Guard Community Rights** and the directions on page 255 aloud. Then instruct each student to fill in the blanks independently, color the pattern, and cut it out. Next, have the student fold the pattern on the thin line and glue the back of the two halves together. If desired, punch a hole at the top of each project and tie a length of yarn through the hole. Use tape to suspend the projects from each student's desk.

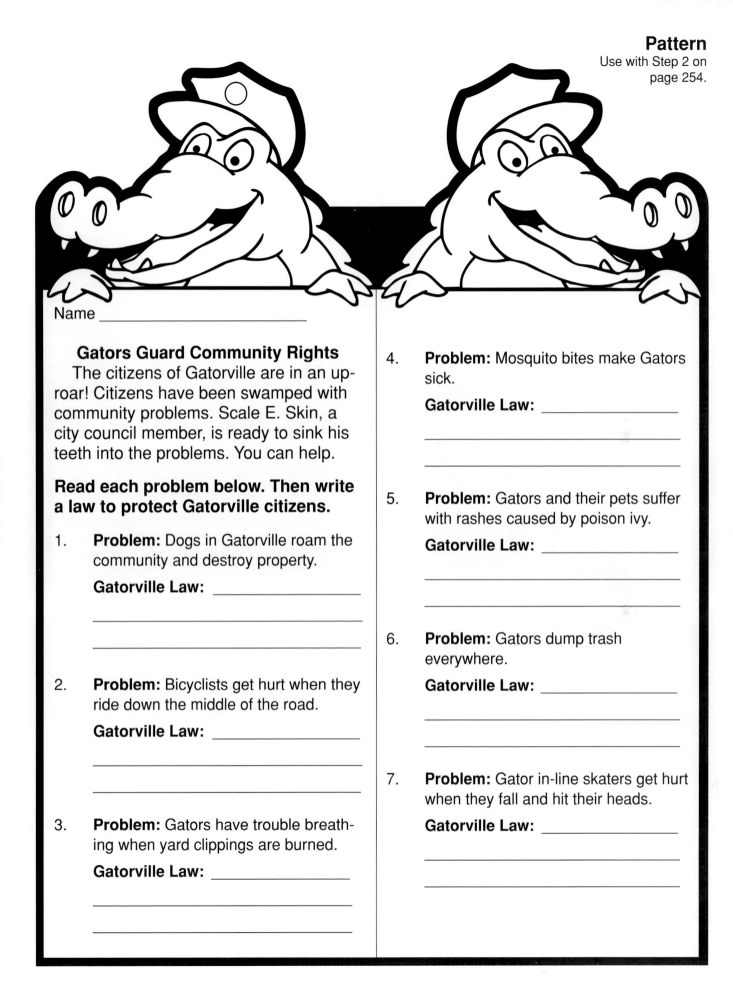

Name _____

Gators Guard Community Rights

The citizens of Gatorville are in an up-roar! Citizens have been swamped with community problems. Scale E. Skin, a city council member, is ready to sink his teeth into the problems. You can help.

Read each problem below. Then write a law to protect Gatorville citizens.

1. **Problem:** Dogs in Gatorville roam the community and destroy property.

   Gatorville Law: _____

   _____

   _____

2. **Problem:** Bicyclists get hurt when they ride down the middle of the road.

   Gatorville Law: _____

   _____

   _____

3. **Problem:** Gators have trouble breath-ing when yard clippings are burned.

   Gatorville Law: _____

   _____

   _____

4. **Problem:** Mosquito bites make Gators sick.

   Gatorville Law: _____

   _____

   _____

5. **Problem:** Gators and their pets suffer with rashes caused by poison ivy.

   Gatorville Law: _____

   _____

   _____

6. **Problem:** Gators dump trash everywhere.

   Gatorville Law: _____

   _____

   _____

7. **Problem:** Gator in-line skaters get hurt when they fall and hit their heads.

   Gatorville Law: _____

   _____

   _____

How To Extend The Lesson:

- Organize students into small groups and have them role-play city leaders considering a proposed law. Write several proposals on the chalkboard, such as "Should adults be required to supervise their children at public parks?" or "Should people with in-line skates be required to pass a safety test before using them in public places?" Instruct each group to select a proposal to discuss. After an appropriate amount of time, have each group report its recommendations to the class.

- Instruct each student to think of a law—serious or funny—to propose to city leaders. Examples of some laws may include that children must not play outside after dark or that all children must eat candy every day. Then have each child write a letter explaining why she thinks her proposal should become law. Allow time for each student volunteer to read her letter aloud and hold a class discussion on the pros and cons of her proposition.

- Invite a city leader, such as a city council member, to visit your classroom. Ask him or her to discuss how laws are made in your community, which laws have been made most recently, and which ones have become outdated due to changes in the community. Encourage students to ask your guest to explain any laws that they don't fully understand.

Why do we have a city ordinance that does not permit a household to hold more than two yard sales a year?

Count On Your Community

Teach youngsters that rights and responsibilities go hand in hand to create a top-notch community.

Skill: Identifying rights and responsibilities of a good citizen

Estimated Lesson Time: 40 minutes

Teacher Preparation:
Duplicate page 259 for each student.

Materials:
1 copy of page 259 for each student
scissors
glue

Background Information:
Citizens must take on certain responsibilities to make a community safe and peaceful. All citizens are responsible for obeying laws, paying taxes, voting in elections, and helping those who are in need. When citizens work together in a community, they make it a better place to live.

GOVERNMENT & CITIZENSHIP

Introducing The Lesson:

Have students name workers they see in school, such as teachers and cafeteria workers. Record their responses on the chalkboard. Next ask students what might happen if these workers did not do their work.

Steps:

1. Encourage students to discuss the ways these people work together each day. Reinforce that students have a right to an education and that everyone—school staff and students—must work together to have a successful school day.

2. Explain to students that people in a *community* also have certain rights and responsibilities. Share the Background Information on page 257 with students.

3. Write the words *rights* and *responsibilities* on the chalkboard. Under the word *rights,* list places such as parks, libraries, schools, and youth centers. Point out to students that all citizens have a right to enjoy these places. Ask students to name the responsibilities involved in having these places in a community (see the suggestions below). Record responses on the chalkboard.

4. Distribute scissors, glue, and a copy of page 259 to each student.

5. Ask a volunteer read the speech bubbles and the directions at the top of the page. Have students complete the page independently.

6. Challenge students to complete the Bonus Box.

rights	responsibilities
parks	pay taxes put litter in its place
libraries	handle books with care pay taxes
schools	treat students and school staff with respect come to school ready to learn
youth centers	treat equipment and property with respect follow the rules

Count On Your Community

Everyone in a community has certain rights and responsibilities.

It is your **responsibility** to keep your community safe and happy.

You have a **right** to enjoy a safe and happy place to live.

Read each sentence.
Cut out each sentence and glue it under the correct heading.

My Community Rights	**My Community Responsibilities**

Bonus Box: On the back of this paper, write five things you could do to be a responsible citizen.

I play at a neighborhood park.	I recycle materials.
I put litter in its correct place.	I can count on others if I need help.
I follow safety rules.	I check out books from the library.
I feel safe in my neighborhood.	I keep my dog from roaming the community.
I help others in need.	I live in a caring community.

How To Extend The Lesson:

- Share with students *Roxaboxen* by Alice McLerran (Puffin Books, 1992), the story of an imaginative community. Point out how the children in the story work together to build a community complete with a mayor and police officers. Ask students to identify the rights and responsibilities described in the story. Then extend the lesson by having small groups of students create imaginative communities of their own. Provide materials such as shoeboxes, clean milk cartons, construction paper, craft sticks, pebbles, scissors, and glue. If desired, have students fashion wooden clothespin people to populate their communities. Encourage each group to include the buildings and people needed to make the community a good place to live. Allow students time to share their completed projects with one another.

- Have students make posters encouraging citizens to act responsibly. Provide each student with crayons and a sheet of white construction paper. Instruct each child to focus on a responsibility that is of concern in her community. Display the completed projects in the hallway for everyone to see.

- Make a student-generated chart to show how community responsibilities are delegated. To do this, write the words *mayor, city council, judge, police officers, citizens,* and *visitors* on the left side of a large sheet of chart paper. Have students describe the responsibilities of each person while you record their responses on the chart (see the example below). Display the completed chart in the classroom for reference during your study of communities.

Our Community

mayor: leader of the city or town
city council: helps make community laws
judge: decides consequences for lawbreakers
police officers: help keep people safe
citizens: follow community rules and help others
visitors: follow rules of the community

Put It To A Vote!

Guide your young voters through a mock election with this award-winning lesson!

Skill: Taking part in democratic decision making

Estimated Lesson Time: 45 minutes

Teacher Preparation:

1. Duplicate page 263 for each student, plus two extras.
2. Color and cut out the two extra campaign ribbons and discard the ballots. Make sure each ribbon is colored differently.
3. Set up a private area for voting in the classroom.
4. Obtain a box or container to serve as a ballot box.

Materials:

1 copy of page 263 for each student
2 differently colored campaign ribbons
ballot box
scissors
crayons
tape

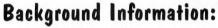

Background Information:

In the United States, every citizen has the right to vote. When it is time to choose new candidates or laws, an election is held. Many citizens go to places called *polls* to cast their votes.

In some elections, people mark a *ballot*—a sheet of paper used to cast a secret vote. A voter goes into a private voting booth and places a mark next to his choice on the ballot; then he places his ballot in the ballot box. In some cases, a voting machine is used instead of a paper ballot. After everyone has had a chance to vote, the votes are counted and the outcome is announced.

Introducing The Lesson:

Begin the lesson by taping the two colored ribbons to the chalkboard. Label one ribbon *A* and the other *B*. Inform the class that later in the lesson each student will vote for the ribbon of his choice.

Steps:

1. Explain that one of the most important parts of an election is the *campaign* that occurs beforehand. In a campaign, some people try to convince voters which way to vote. Instruct students to choose a ribbon and write a campaign slogan for it, such as "Green, red, and blue is the ribbon for you!" Have students read their slogans aloud; then encourage students to decide which ribbon they prefer.

2. Ask students to put their heads down for privacy. Have them raise their hands for choice A or B. Then tally the votes on the chalkboard. If there is a tie, add your vote to the results.

3. Have students look at the results. Explain that the choice with the most votes is the winner by *majority rule,* because more than half of the class voted for it. Share the Background Information on page 261 with students. Remove the ribbons from the chalkboard.

4. Inform students that they will vote for other colors to be used in new campaign ribbons. Distribute a copy of page 263 and a pair of scissors to each student. Then instruct each child to cut out his ballot. Have each student cast his vote by marking one box in each section; then have him place his ballot in the ballot box.

5. While students are voting, write the six categories and their choices on the chalkboard. Enlist students' help in tallying the votes. Have students color their ribbons according to the election results. Then have students cut out and wear their ribbons.

Put It To A Vote!

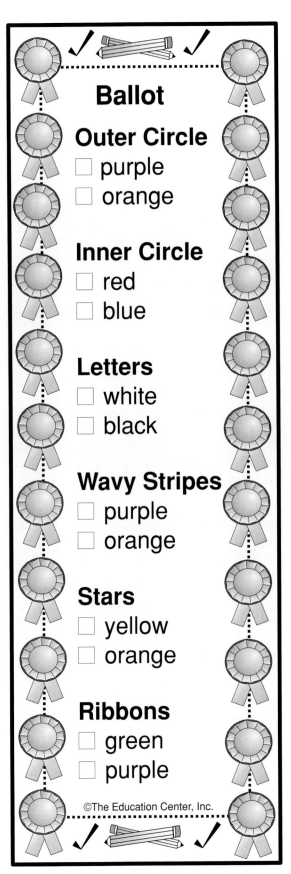

Ballot

Outer Circle
☐ purple
☐ orange

Inner Circle
☐ red
☐ blue

Letters
☐ white
☐ black

Wavy Stripes
☐ purple
☐ orange

Stars
☐ yellow
☐ orange

Ribbons
☐ green
☐ purple

©The Education Center, Inc.

How To Extend The Lesson:

- Explain to students that voters must meet certain requirements in order to vote. A voter must be at least 18 years of age, a citizen of the United States, and registered to vote. A registered voter is given a voter registration card. Obtain a few real voter registration cards for students to examine; then have students make their own voter registration cards to be used for classroom voting.

- Organize students into small groups to create a class mascot. Have each group discuss what its mascot will look like and decide upon a name for it. Next, instruct each group to list five characteristics that would make its mascot a good choice, and then draw a picture of it. Have each group campaign for its mascot in front of another class. After each group has given its campaign speech, hold an election to vote for the new mascot. Allow both classes to vote and hear the results of the election. Display the pictures of all mascots in a prominent location in your classroom.

- Have each student write a list of three topics on which the class could vote, such as which book to be read aloud or which game to play during the next indoor recess. Collect the lists and choose one topic. Program one copy of the ballot below with the topic and the choices on which to vote. Then duplicate a class set of the ballot and have students vote. If desired, have each student show her voter registration card before voting (see the first idea on this page). Repeat the activity in a similar manner with other topics.

Ballot

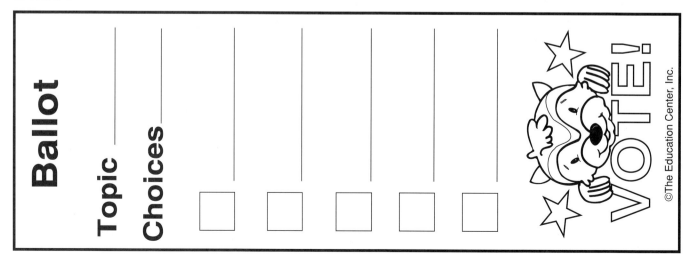

A Star-Spangled Tour

Send students on a trip to see impressive U.S. monuments and landforms—without leaving their seats!

Skill: Identifying significant U.S. monuments and landforms

Estimated Lesson Time: 45 minutes

Teacher Preparation:

1. Duplicate page 267 for each student.
2. Program a set of index cards as shown below.

Materials:

1 copy of page 267 for each student
one 12" x 18" sheet of light-colored
  construction paper for each student
set of programmed index cards
large United States map
scissors
glue
crayons
tape

Background Information:

    Many famous U.S. landforms are known for their natural beauty. The Grand Canyon is a spectacular gorge in Arizona and the Everglades are beautiful marshlands in southern Florida.

    U.S. monuments honor our nation and remind us of the freedoms we enjoy. Mount Rushmore National Memorial is a huge sculpture in South Dakota that honors four U.S. presidents. The Statue of Liberty is a sculpture that towers above Liberty Island in New York and has become a symbol of freedom.

insect repellent	camera with wide-angle lens	binoculars	tennis shoes
There's plenty of bugs buzzing in this watery place!	These four famous faces are so large it will take a special lens to take their picture!	This place is deep and wide, and there's a lot to see!	You'll need a good pair of shoes to climb to the top of this monument!

Introducing The Lesson:

Tell students you are going to take them on a trip across the United States to visit famous monuments and landforms. Then draw a large outline of a suitcase on the chalkboard. Post the programmed index cards (item-side facing up) inside the suitcase. Next write the names of each monument or landform around the suitcase. Explain to students that they will need the items in the suitcase for an imaginary visit to important U.S. monuments and landforms.

Steps:

1. Remove the card with the word *binoculars* on it. Then read the back of the card aloud. Ask students to guess which U.S. landform they are visiting. Confirm that it is the Grand Canyon. Point to its location (Arizona) on the United States map.

2. Repeat the procedure as you remove each card from the suitcase, locating Mount Rushmore in South Dakota, the Statue of Liberty in New York, and the Everglades in Florida.

3. Tell students that now that the trip has been completed, each child will create a photo album page featuring these U.S. monuments and landforms.

4. Distribute a 12" x 18" sheet of light-colored construction paper, scissors, crayons, glue, and a copy of page 267 to each student.

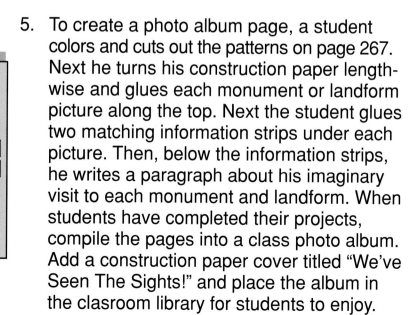

5. To create a photo album page, a student colors and cuts out the patterns on page 267. Next he turns his construction paper length-wise and glues each monument or landform picture along the top. Next the student glues two matching information strips under each picture. Then, below the information strips, he writes a paragraph about his imaginary visit to each monument and landform. When students have completed their projects, compile the pages into a class photo album. Add a construction paper cover titled "We've Seen The Sights!" and place the album in the classroom library for students to enjoy.

Mount Rushmore

Grand Canyon

Everglades

Statue of Liberty

These marshlands, found in Florida, have plains of grass and trees.

It's a long way to the top! From its feet to the tip of its torch, this sculpture is over 150 feet high.

Carved by the Colorado River, this hole in the ground is over one mile deep in places.

You'll find a variety of wildlife here including alligators, cougars, manatees, and many birds.

This huge sculpture of four U.S. presidents is found in the Black Hills of South Dakota.

What a popular place! Each year about two million people visit this statue of a robed woman.

These four faces are George Washington, Thomas Jefferson, Theodore Roosevelt, and Abraham Lincoln.

At sunset the red and brown layers in this canyon's walls are a beautiful sight.

How To Extend The Lesson:

- Have each student select and research a famous U.S. landform or monument. Assign or, if desired, have each student select a landform or monument (refer to the list below). Provide references, such as encyclopedias and books, for the student to use to research her topic. Next, on a large sheet of construction paper, have the student draw an illustration of her landform or monument and list several interesting facts about it, including its location. Display the completed posters in the hallway as a tribute to our country's national treasures.

Niagara Falls
Yellowstone National Park
Washington Monument
Lincoln Memorial
Carlsbad Caverns National Park

Pikes Peak
Great Salt Lake
Mojave Desert
The Gateway Arch
Vietnam Veterans Memorial

- Tap into your students' creativity by turning your classroom into a souvenir shop. Supply students with construction paper, markers, sequins, yarn, glue, and other art materials. Then assign each pair of students a different famous American landform or monument. Instruct students to create souvenirs—such as postcards, bumper stickers, pennants, jewelry, posters, and maps—to represent their assigned topics. When students have finished the assignment, have each pair present its completed inventory to the class, describing each souvenir. Then keep the items on display throughout your study of landforms and monuments.

My mountain has the tallest peak in the U.S. What am I?

Mount McKinley

I am an amazing waterfall. What am I?

Niagra Falls

I am a statue of our 16ᵗʰ president. What am I?

Lincoln Memorial

- Play "American Places Pursuit" as a class guessing game. Give each child an index card. Have her select a famous landform or monument that has been studied in class, then follow the samples shown to write a "What Am I?" riddle about it. Have her write the answer at the bottom of the card. Next collect the cards and place them in a container. Then divide the class into two teams. In turn, one member from each team takes a card and reads it to the other team. Award a point for each correct answer.

Letter-Perfect Leaders

When it comes to learning about leaders, this first-class lesson really delivers!

> **Skill:** Recognizing the roles of local, state, and national leaders

Estimated Lesson Time: 30 minutes

Teacher Preparation:
1. Draw three large, concentric circles on the chalkboard.
2. Duplicate page 271 for each student.

Materials:
1 copy of page 271 per student
scissors
glue

Background Information:
Government in the United States has three levels—local, state, and national. Each level has a leader who works to meet the needs and wants of the people in his community: the citizens. The local, state, and national leaders are the mayor, governor, and president of the United States, respectively. Each leader's role in the community is described below.

• Mayor
—Works in city hall
—Helps establish city laws and make sure that they are followed
—Manages the libraries and the police, fire, transportation, and sanitation departments at the local level

• Governor
—Works in the state capitol
—Helps establish state laws and make sure that they are followed
—Manages education, public safety, recreation, welfare, and conservation at the state level

• President of the United States
—Works in the White House in Washington, DC
—Helps establish federal laws and make sure that they are followed
—Acts as the Commander in Chief of the Army, Navy, Air Force, and Marines
—Determines U.S. relations with other nations

Introducing The Lesson:

Direct students' attention to the circles on the board. Explain that the circles represent three communities to which each of them belong. Write "Local" in the smallest circle. Tell youngsters that their town or city is the local community. Ask youngsters to identify a larger community of which their town or city is part. Verify that their town or city is part of the state community; then write "State" on the next larger circle. Lead youngsters to name the community to which the state belongs—the nation—and write "National" on the largest circle. Tell students that they will learn about the job of each community's leader.

Steps:

1. Beginning with the local community, use the Background Information on page 269 to identify the leader of each community represented on the chalkboard and to describe his role.

2. Ask youngsters to identify similarities and differences among the roles of the three leaders discussed.

3. Tell students that it is important for citizens to let their leaders know how they feel about community issues. Name several topics that affect communities, such as building a new city library, protecting a state park, or establishing a national school curriculum. Ask students to identify the leader with whom it would be most appropriate to discuss each topic.

4. Explain that many citizens share their opinions and ideas with community leaders by writing letters to them. Tell youngsters that for this activity, they will imagine they are writing letters to a mayor, a governor, and the president. Give each student a copy of page 271, a pair of scissors, and glue. Have him cut out the envelopes on the dotted lines, then follow the directions on his sheet.

5. Challenge students to complete the Bonus Box activity.

Letter-Perfect Leaders

For each topic, decide who would be the best community leader to write. Glue an envelope beside each topic to show your answer.

1. building a bigger and better city library

2. an idea for a new national song

3. cutting down a forest so that the state highway can be made bigger

4. a state law that would make the school year longer

5. adding a baseball diamond to the city park

6. City Council's plan to outlaw bike riding after 4:00 P.M.

7. making a new holiday called National Bubble Gum Day

8. changing the state license plate design

Bonus Box: On the back of this sheet, list three things you would do if you were the governor.

| Mayor | Mayor | Mayor | Governor | Governor | Governor | President | President |

How To Extend The Lesson:

- Use this bulletin-board idea to extend students' learning about leaders. Tack two lengths of yarn on the board to visually divide it into three equal-size columns. Mount cards labeled "Local," "State," and "National" at the top of the columns. On each of several days, provide students with newspapers. Have students cut out articles about issues at each of these levels. Mount articles related to the mayor's, governor's, and president's roles on red, white, and blue paper, respectively. Staple them onto the board in the appropriate columns. After an article is added to the display, read it aloud and discuss the issue featured.

- This class activity is perfect for reviewing the jobs of government leaders! On each of several slips of paper, write a different clue about the job of a mayor, governor, or the president. For example, write "works in the state capitol" as a clue for governor. Fold each slip and place it in a container. Give each student three index cards. Have him label his cards "Mayor," "Governor," and "President." To begin, take a strip from the container and read it aloud. Ask each student to identify which leader the clue describes by holding up his corresponding card. Look at the raised cards to check students' accuracy. Ask a youngster who is holding the correct card to name the leader. Continue with a desired number of additional clues in a like manner.

- Reinforce students' understanding of local, state, and national leaders' jobs with this step booklet project. To make his booklet, each youngster needs a 7" x 10" piece of red construction paper, a 9" x 12" piece of white construction paper, and a 12" x 15" piece of blue construction paper. He folds each paper in half; then staples the white and red papers atop the blue paper as shown. The youngster labels the red paper "Mayor," the white paper "Governor," and the blue paper "President." Next he describes each leader's job on a separate piece of writing paper sized to fit the corresponding page of his booklet. Finally, the student glues each description onto the appropriate page. Invite each youngster to share his work, and then tell which of the three jobs he would most like to have and why.

Mayor

Governor

President

Ready, Set, Race!

Students will "purr-fect" their understanding of cardinal and intermediate directions with these two cool cats!

Skill: Using cardinal and intermediate directions

Estimated Lesson Time: 40 minutes

Teacher Preparation:
1. Duplicate page 275 for each student.
2. Label each wall or corner in your classroom with the appropriate cardinal or intermediate direction.
3. Draw a grid (like the one shown on page 274) on the chalkboard.

Materials:
1 copy of page 275 for each student
8 labeled signs

Background Information:
The four *cardinal directions* are north, south, east, and west. These directions are represented by the letters *N, S, E,* and *W* on a *compass rose*. A compass rose indicates directions on a map.

Intermediate directions are located halfway between the cardinal directions on a compass rose. The intermediate directions are northeast (NE), southeast (SE), southwest (SW), and northwest (NW).

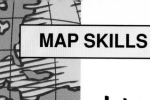

Introducing The Lesson:

Ask students what type of activities might require the use of a compass. Accept responses such as hiking or sailing. Then explain to students that a map has a compass called a compass rose. Next share the Background Information on page 273 with students. Then draw a simple compass rose on the chalkboard and label the cardinal and intermediate directions.

Steps:

1. Refer students to the cardinal and intermediate directions on the classroom walls. Direct students to stand, face the north wall, and quietly march in place. Announce a direction and have students turn and face that direction while marching in place. Call out another direction, giving students time to change directions. Continue in this same manner until students demonstrate an understanding of cardinal and intermediate directions. Then ask students to return to their seats.

2. Draw a flower in one of the boxes of the grid, and a star in another box. Announce a direction, such as "Go north two boxes." Instruct a student volunteer to start at the flower and draw a chalk line according to your oral directions. When the student has completed the first step, have other students follow similar oral directions until the line reaches the star. Then erase the flower, star, and line. Redraw the star and flower in different boxes. Repeat the process until students have a good understanding of using directions on a grid.

3. Distribute a copy of page 275 to each student. Review the directions with students and have each child complete the page independently.

4. Challenge students to complete the Bonus Box activity.

Ready, Set, Race!

Read the clues below the grid.
Draw the paths Casey and Smitty take to the stuffed mouse.
Then answer the question below.

Begin at the pawprint marked (S) for Smitty .
1. Go south 2 blocks.
2. Go southeast 3 blocks.
3. Go southwest 1 block.
4. Go south 3 blocks.
5. Go northeast 2 blocks.
6. Go east 4 blocks.

Begin at the pawprint marked (C) for Casey.
1. Go north 2 blocks.
2. Go northwest 2 blocks.
3. Go west 2 blocks.
4. Go northwest 3 blocks.
5. Go west 2 blocks.
6. Go south 2 blocks.

Which cat got to the stuffed mouse? _____

Bonus Box: Draw a path for a third cat. Start the cat's path at the heart in the upper right-hand corner of the grid. Change directions at least three times. Finish the path at the stuffed mouse. On another sheet of paper, write the directions of the path.

How To Extend The Lesson:

- Students demonstrate their understanding of cardinal and intermediate directions with this engaging game. Have eight students stand in a circle, facing center. Tell the class to imagine the eight children are standing on a compass rose. Review the cardinal or intermediate direction that each of the eight children represents. Next ask a seated child to stand in the center of the circle and face north. Then ask the child in the center a question, such as "Who is standing northwest of you?" If the response is correct, the northwest student confirms it. Then the child in the center chooses a seated student to take his place. If the response is incorrect, the child in the center and the northwest student trade places. Continue in this manner until all students have had a chance to participate in some aspect of the game.

- When students are out of the classroom, hide a small object such as a stuffed mouse or a chalkboard eraser. Guide a student volunteer to the item by giving her a series of directional clues, such as "Take five giant steps northwest." Continue giving clues until she has found the item. Have another student volunteer cover his eyes as you hide the item in a different location. Have the student uncover his eyes and play the game again.

- Duplicate page 275 and cut out the grid. Then duplicate a copy of the grid for each student. Instruct the student to write a set of directional clues for Casey and Smitty, changing directions at least four times. After all students have completed the assignment, have them exchange papers and mark the paths according to the directions. Then have each student return his paper to its original owner to be checked.

Begin at the S pawprint.
1. Go east 6 blocks.
2. Go south 8 blocks
3. Go east 9 blocks
4. Go north west 3 blocks.

Blasting Off With Grids

Launch your study of grids with this far-reaching unit!

Skill: Using a grid

Estimated Lesson Time: 45 minutes

Teacher Preparation:
1. Duplicate page 279 for each student.
2. Label each of six sheets of construction paper with one of the following letters or numerals: *A, B, C, 1, 2,* and *3* (one letter or numeral per sheet).
3. Using masking tape, create a 3 x 3 grid on the classroom floor. Each box needs to be large enough for a person to stand in.

Materials:
1 copy of page 279 for each student
masking tape
6 sheets of construction paper
marker

I'm at B4.
Beam me up!

Background Information:
A *grid* is a set of crossing vertical and horizontal lines used to locate places on a map. The lines form boxes that make it easier to describe a location on a map. *Rows* are the boxes arranged horizontally. *Columns* are the boxes arranged vertically.

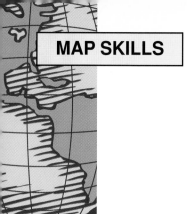

Introducing The Lesson:

Instruct students to gather around the grid on the floor. Have six student volunteers each hold a labeled sheet of construction paper. Direct each student with a numeral to sit beside a row. Then direct each student with a letter to sit above a column as shown. Keep the letters and numerals in order.

Steps:

1. Stand in one of the boxes. Ask a volunteer to describe where you are standing. Accept any reasonable response. Then share the Background Information on page 277.

2. Explain that the letters and numbers work together to determine a specific box on the grid. Point to the child in your column and to the child in your row. Have the pair hold up their cards. Announce the coordinates.

3. Stand in a different box and repeat Step 2 until students have an understanding of how the grid works. Then have students return to their seats.

4. Distribute a copy of page 279 to each child.

5. Review the directions at the top of the page. Reinforce the use of the grid by asking where the space traveler would go for shuttle repairs and confirm the response *(to the garage in E2).* Have students complete the page independently.

6. Challenge students to complete the Bonus Box activity.

I am standing in C2.

Blasting Off With Grids

Space traveler Red E. Tolaunch has just landed at Sparky's Space Station. She plans to run a few errands and get some much needed rest before she blasts off to another galaxy. However, Red needs help with her map. Use the grid to write the location of each place on Red's list.

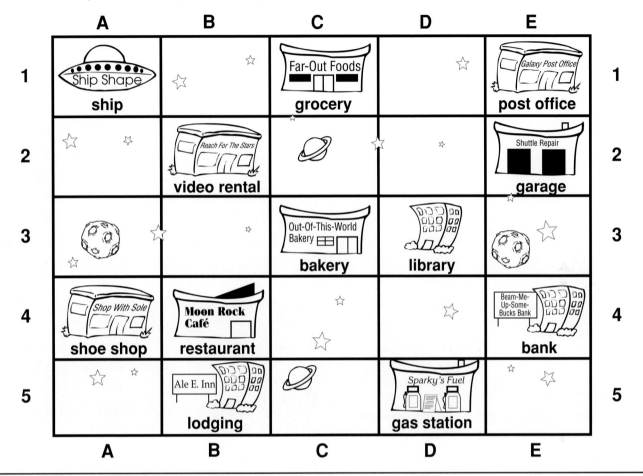

List Of Errands

1. Return the book *No Longer Lost In Space* to Stellar Library. _____
2. Pick up mail at the Galaxy Post Office. _____
3. Eat a fine meal at Moon Rock Café. _____
4. Pick up some groceries at Far-Out Foods. _____
5. Get some cash at Beam-Me-Up-Some-Bucks Bank. _____
6. Enjoy some donuts at Out-Of-This-World Bakery. _____
7. Have the hole in my spaceshoe repaired at Shop With Sole. _____
8. Get a good night's sleep at Ale E. Inn. _____
9. I need to return something at B2. What could it be? _____
10. Oh, no! Where did I park my spaceship, *Ship Shape?* _____

Bonus Box: Red forgot to write down something she needs! She can't blast off without it! Look at the map. On the back of this paper, write what Red needs to get and where she can get it.

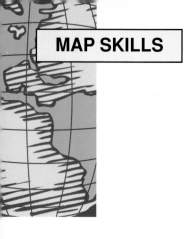

How To Extend The Lesson:

- Invite students to add a creative touch to their grid practice. In advance, create a 10 x 10 grid and duplicate a copy for each student, plus one extra. On the extra grid create a simple design similar to the one shown below. Then, on the chalkboard, make a list of the boxes that have been filled in to create the design. To complete the activity, each student refers to the list and colors the appropriate boxes on her grid. After each student has completed her design, post the original design for students to check their papers. If desired, duplicate extra copies of the blank grid and encourage each student to create her own design, list the boxes to color, and then ask a classmate to solve it.

- Using a grid pattern such as the one suggested above, instruct students to design a playground. Have each student draw playground equipment in the boxes of his choice. Then have students exchange papers and write the location of each piece of equipment.

- Gather a collection of timetables that are displayed in a grid, such as train schedules, bus schedules, or schedules of television programs. Have students apply their understanding of grids to determine arrival and departure times or the times of certain television programs.

- Use a globe or map of the world to show how latitude and longitude lines create a grid. Have students locate different countries using these lines.

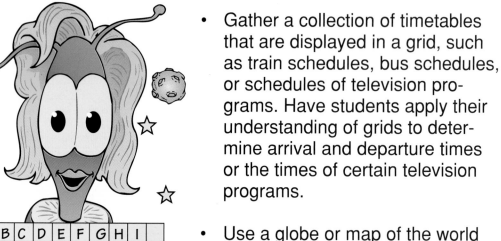

Color the following boxes:

1. H2	9. D5
2. E3	10. F5
3. G3	11. B6
4. I3	12. D6
5. E4	13. A7
6. F4	14. C7
7. H4	15. A8
8. B5	16. C8

Homegrown

Students discover that product maps are a picture-perfect learning tool with this lesson!

Skill: Analyzing a product map

Estimated Lesson Time: 30 minutes

Teacher Preparation:
1. Duplicate page 283 for each student.
2. Cut out or draw several pictures of well-known agricultural products, such as oranges, coconuts, rice, or maple syrup.

Materials:
1 copy of page 283 for each student
several pictures of well-known agricultural products
a large United States and/or world map (optional)
crayons (optional)

Background Information:
A product map uses symbols to show the location of the most important products of an area. Symbols are explained in the map key.

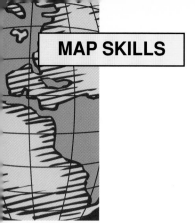

Introducing The Lesson:

Begin the lesson by displaying the pictures of well-known agricultural products. Ask students to guess where the products were grown. Accept all reasonable responses.

Steps:

1. Share the Background Information on page 281. Then distribute a copy of page 283 to each student. Explain to students that the reproducible shows a product map of an area where people make a living raising crops.

2. Instruct each student to locate the map key on her reproducible. Call on student volunteers to share the information found in the map key. If desired, have students lightly color each symbol (both in the key and on the map) a different color to help distinguish between them.

3. Guide students in understanding that a product map gives us information about the crops of an area and gives clues as to the types of jobs available there. For example, the types of jobs available where oranges are grown might include farming, orange picking, and making orange juice or orange marmalade.

4. Review the directions at the top of the page and have each student complete the page independently.

5. Challenge students to complete the Bonus Box activity.

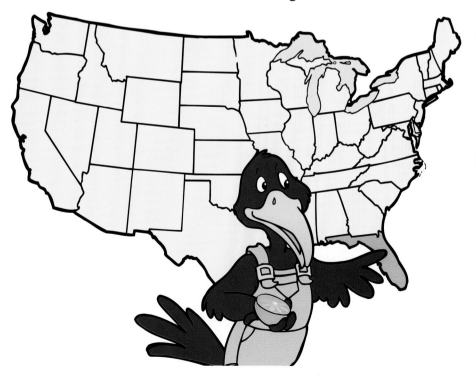

Homegrown

Read the questions below.
Then use the product map to help answer the questions.
Write your answers on the lines.

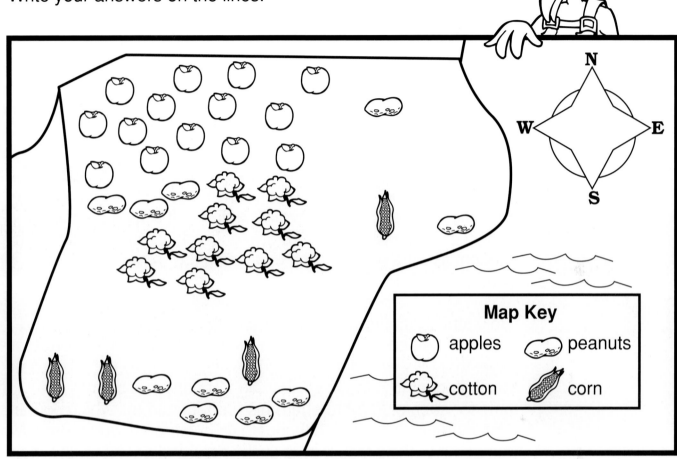

1. What is used to show products on a map? _____
2. How many different products are shown on the map? _____
3. Which product is grown the most? _____
4. In how many different places are peanuts grown? _____
5. Which product is found the most in the northern part of the state? _____
6. Which two products are grown in the southern part of the state? _____
    _____
7. Which product is grown in the north, south, east, and west of the state?
    _____
8. Which crops are grown in the center of the state? _____
9. Which crop is grown as much as cotton? _____
10. Which product probably brings in the least amount of money? _____
    Why? _____

Bonus Box: On the back of this paper, list three jobs that might be found in this state.

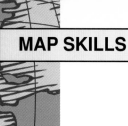
How To Extend The Lesson:

- Have students create their own product maps with this engaging lesson. For each of several small groups, draw a large outline of your state on a sheet of tagboard. Then provide each group with a state outline, crayons, and reference materials containing product information about your state. Then instruct each group to create a product map within the state outline that shows the important agricultural areas. Instruct each group to include a key on its product map. Post the completed maps on a classroom wall for everyone to see.

- Arrange a field trip to a place where an important agricultural or industrial product is made in your town. Have students observe the different types of jobs available due to the type of product grown or made. When you return to the classroom, direct each student to write a paragraph explaining the importance of the product to the local community.

- Help students understand that more than just agricultural products can be shown on a product map. Show students a product's label that tells where it was made, such as a sweater. Then ask each student to bring in something from another country. Provide time for each student to share his product and tell which country it was made in; then help him locate its origin on a world map. Write the name of the product on a sticky note and post it on the map. After everyone has shared, discuss the information on the map.

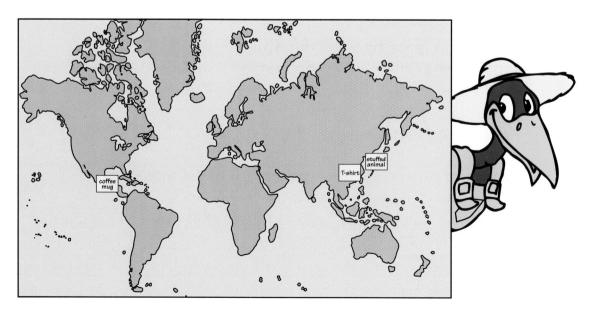

A Bird's-Eye View Of Geography

Take students' understanding of geographic terms to new heights with this high-flying lesson!

Skill: Identifying and describing geographic terms

Estimated Lesson Time: 45 minutes

Teacher Preparation:

1. Duplicate page 287 and the bird's-eye view diagram on page 288 for each student.
2. Cut out ten construction-paper fish. On each fish, write one of the geographic terms listed in the Background Information below.

Materials:

1 copy of page 287 and the bird's-eye view diagram on page 288 for each student
10 construction-paper fish labeled with geographic terms
tape

Background Information:

The earth is covered with a variety of land and water features. Some of the features are:

ocean—a large body of salt water
coast—the land next to the ocean
harbor—a place on a coast where ships can dock safely
gulf—a large area of ocean partly surrounded by land
bay—a small area of ocean partly surrounded by land
island—land completely surrounded by water
peninsula—a piece of land with water on three sides of it
river—a large stream of water
delta—the land formed at the mouth of a river
mouth of river—the place where a river empties into a larger body of water

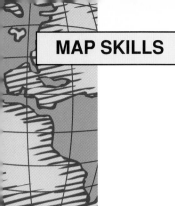
Introducing The Lesson:

On the chalkboard, draw a pelican with a large bill like the one shown below. Then draw a wavy line across the board to indicate water and tape the ten construction-paper fish below it. Announce to students that "Big Bill," a very hungry pelican, is ready for a snack! Explain that they will catch fish for him.

Steps:

1. Give each student a copy of the bird's-eye view diagram on page 288. To have students catch a fish for Big Bill, read a definition of one of the terms from the Background Information (page 285). Then ask a volunteer to take down the fish that is labeled with the word that matches the definition. If the student selects the correct word, he tapes the fish in the pelican's bill. If the student's choice is incorrect, he returns the fish to the ocean and tries again. After a correct response, have each student write the term on the appropriate line on his diagram. Continue in this manner until all the fish have been fed to Big Bill.

2. Give each student a copy of page 287. Review the directions and have each student complete the page independently.

3. Challenge students to complete the Bonus Box activity.

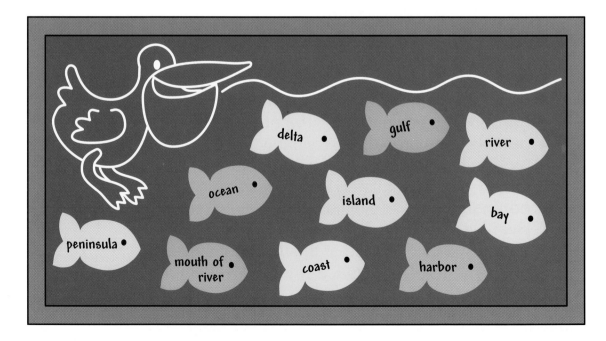

A Bird's-Eye View Of Geography

Read each definition in Big Bill's bill.
Find the fish with the matching word.
Write the fish's letter on the blank.

1. _____ a piece of land with water on three sides of it
2. _____ a large area of ocean partly surrounded by land
3. _____ a small area of ocean partly surrounded by land
4. _____ a large stream of water
5. _____ a large body of salt water
6. _____ the place where a river empties into a larger body of water
7. _____ the land next to an ocean
8. _____ land completely surrounded by water
9. _____ a place on a coast where ships can dock safely
10. _____ the land formed at the mouth of a river

A. ocean
B. peninsula
C. bay
D. harbor
E. island
F. mouth of river
G. coast
H. gulf
I. delta
J. river

Fill in each blank below with the correct word. Use the words listed on the fish.

1. Airplane is to airport as boat is to _____.
2. Moat is to castle as water is to _____.
3. Cupcake is to cake as bay is to _____.

Bonus Box: On the back of this paper, write a sentence describing the differences between each of the following:
1. peninsula and island
2. bay and gulf

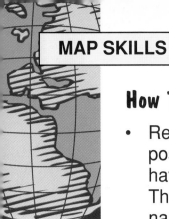
How To Extend The Lesson:

- Reinforce your study of geographic terms by having students create postcards. Give each student a 4" x 6" index card. On the unlined side, have each student color a picture of one of the natural features studied. Then direct the student to turn her card over and write about an imaginary visit to the area, being sure to include the name of the natural feature and a description. Next have her address her card to a classmate before delivering it to him or her.

- Use this center activity to review geographic terms and encourage critical thinking. Create a set of vocabulary cards with the geographic terms studied. Place the cards, a supply of paper, a pencil, and two Hula Hoop® rings at a center. To complete the activity, a student places the rings on the floor next to each other. Then he determines classifications for some of the words, such as land versus water, large versus small, or coastal versus inland. Next he places the cards with words that fit one classification into one ring and the cards with words that fit the other classification into the other ring. Then he writes down the different classifications and the corresponding geographic terms. When finished, he shares his lists with a classmate.

Bird's-Eye View

Use with Step 1 on page 286.

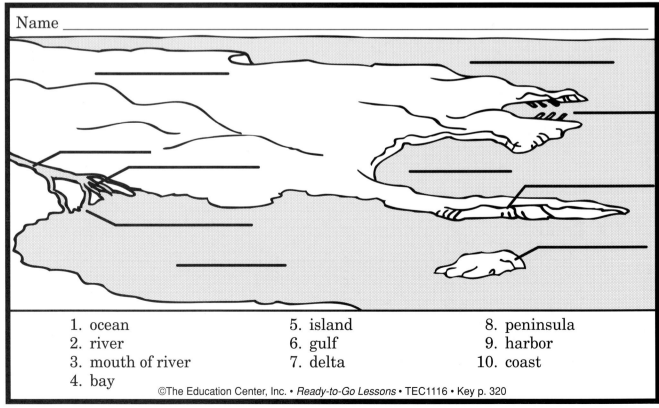

Name _____

1. ocean	5. island	8. peninsula
2. river	6. gulf	9. harbor
3. mouth of river	7. delta	10. coast
4. bay		

©The Education Center, Inc. • *Ready-to-Go Lessons* • TEC1116 • Key p. 320

Where In The World?

Send students searching for the earth's continents and oceans with this worldly lesson.

Skill: Identifying continents and oceans

Estimated Lesson Time: 30 minutes

Teacher Preparation:

1. Duplicate page 291 for each student.
2. Use the chart below to label each of 11 index cards.

Front Of Card	Back Of Card
North America	suitcase
South America	hat
Europe	umbrella
Asia	alarm clock
Antarctica	boots
Africa	backpack
Australia	toothbrush
Atlantic Ocean	swimming trunks
Pacific Ocean	suntan lotion
Indian Ocean	sunglasses
Arctic Ocean	socks

Materials:

1 copy of page 291 for each student
11 index cards labeled with
   continents and oceans
crayons

Background Information:

The earth's large land areas are called *continents*. There are seven continents. They are North America, South America, Europe, Asia, Antarctica, Africa, and Australia.

Our world has four oceans. They are the Atlantic, the Pacific, the Indian, and the Arctic. The largest is the Pacific Ocean and the smallest is the Arctic Ocean.

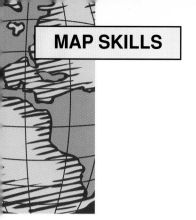

Introducing The Lesson:

Ask students if they have ever lost anything while traveling. Provide time for students to tell briefly about some of their experiences. Then distribute a copy of page 291 to each student. Tell students that Grizz Lee Bear is a world-traveling bear who has lost many personal possessions on his journeys. Assign the class the task of helping Grizz Lee Bear find them.

Steps:

1. Choose one of the programmed index cards and read aloud the item (not the continent or ocean). Instruct each student to look at her world map on the reproducible and find where Grizz Lee Bear left it. When students have located the item on the map, ask if anyone can name the continent or ocean where it was found. Confirm the answer or provide it by showing the other side of the card. Then instruct each student to label the continent or ocean on her map. Continue in this manner until all continents and oceans have been identified and labeled. If desired, encourage students to lightly color their maps to distinguish between the continents and oceans.

2. Refer students to the compass rose on their maps and review cardinal directions. Then have a volunteer read the directions below the map. Instruct each student to complete the page independently.

3. Challenge students to complete the Bonus Box activity.

Where In The World?

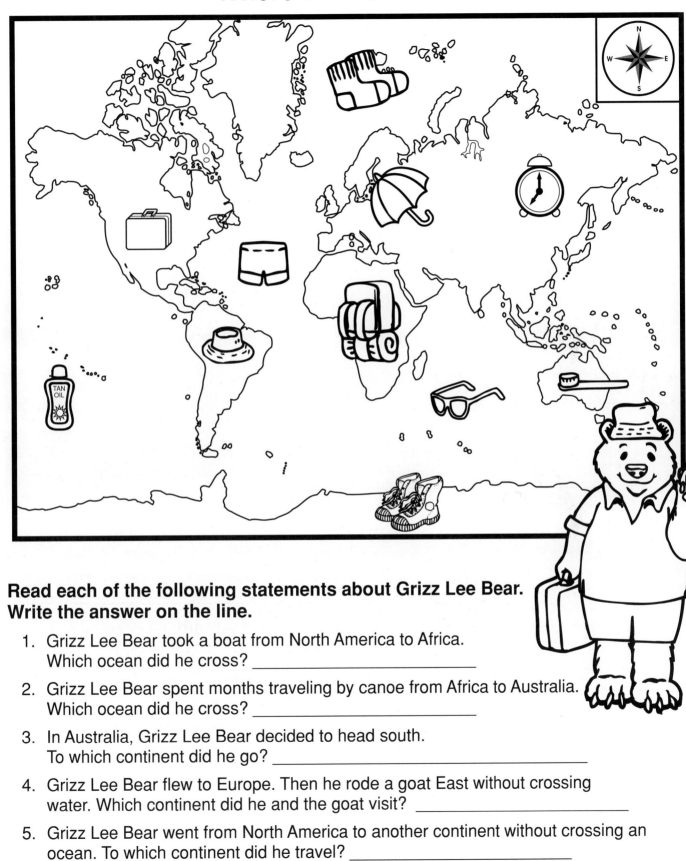

Read each of the following statements about Grizz Lee Bear. Write the answer on the line.

1. Grizz Lee Bear took a boat from North America to Africa. Which ocean did he cross? _____

2. Grizz Lee Bear spent months traveling by canoe from Africa to Australia. Which ocean did he cross? _____

3. In Australia, Grizz Lee Bear decided to head south. To which continent did he go? _____

4. Grizz Lee Bear flew to Europe. Then he rode a goat East without crossing water. Which continent did he and the goat visit? _____

5. Grizz Lee Bear went from North America to another continent without crossing an ocean. To which continent did he travel? _____

Bonus Box: On the back of this paper, write the names of two continents that are joined.

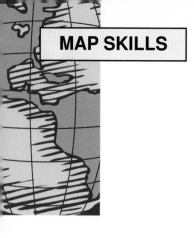

How To Extend The Lesson:

- Display a large world map. Then pair students and assign each twosome a continent or ocean. Instruct each pair to write a riddle about its assigned geographical feature on a sheet of paper. (For example: The Atlantic Ocean and the Indian Ocean touch me. Europe is north of me. Who am I? *[Africa]*) Have students write the answer to the riddle at the bottom of their papers. When students have completed their riddles, collect them and read each one aloud. Challenge student volunteers to determine the answers to the riddles and point to the geographical feature on the map.

- Assign each student a continent or ocean. Provide reference materials, such as encyclopedias, and have the student find several facts about his topic. Then have the student make an acrostic like the one shown that incorporates some of the facts. Invite students to decorate their completed work; then display the acrostics on a bulletin board titled "Words Of The World!"

- Use this center idea to motivate youngsters to practice identifying continents and oceans. Enlarge one copy of the map on page 291. If desired, color and laminate it. With a marker, label 11 pinch clothespins with a different continent or ocean. Place the map, clothespins, and the labeled index cards used for the lesson on page 290 at the center. To complete the activity, the student matches a labeled clothespin to its corresponding continent or ocean on the map (see the illustration on this page). Once all of the clothespins are standing, the student checks his answers against the index cards.

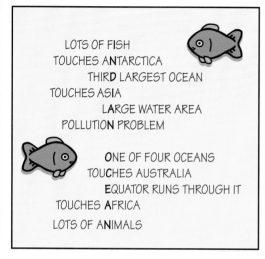

LOTS OF FISH
TOUCHES ANTARCTICA
THIRD LARGEST OCEAN
TOUCHES ASIA
LARGE WATER AREA
POLLUTION PROBLEM

ONE OF FOUR OCEANS
TOUCHES AUSTRALIA
EQUATOR RUNS THROUGH IT
TOUCHES AFRICA
LOTS OF ANIMALS

Going The Distance With Scales

Students will measure up with this map-scale lesson.

Skill: Using a scale to determine distance

Estimated Lesson Time: 30 minutes

Teacher Preparation:
Duplicate page 295 for each student.

Materials:
1 copy of page 295 for each student
1 globe
1 centimeter ruler for each student
scissors
glue

Background Information:

Maps are used to represent real places on the earth's surface. For a map to be manageable, the places and distances shown must be smaller than their actual sizes. For a map to be useful, it must show the correct size of an area and the correct distances between places.

Bar scales are included on maps to help the user determine distances. A bar scale uses a standard unit of measurement, such as an inch, to stand for a certain number of miles or kilometers.

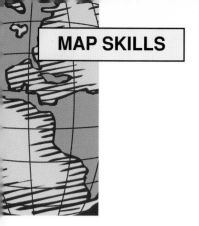

Introducing The Lesson:

Ask students how long it might take to travel all the way around the earth. Discuss the different modes of transportation one might use and which might be fastest. Next proclaim that you can travel around the world in less than one minute. Then place a globe in the front of the room and walk around it.

Steps:

1. Remind students that the globe is a scaled-down model of the earth. Discuss how the landforms on the globe are the correct shapes and distances from one another, but smaller.

2. Ask students to explain the differences between a globe and a map. Accept reasonable responses, such as a globe is like a ball and a map is flat. Then share the Background Information on page 293 with students.

3. Draw a simple bar scale on the chalkboard (see the example at the left). Explain to students that map scales help people determine distances between places.

4. Distribute centimeter rulers, scissors, glue, and a copy of page 295 to each student. Tell students that Marty Mountaineer is vacationing at Grande National Park but his map is incomplete. Marty needs their help filling in the missing information. Read the directions aloud and, if desired, complete the first clue together. Then have students complete the page independently.

5. Challenge students to complete the Bonus Box activity.

Bar Scale

0   1

1 inch = 1 mile

Name_____

Going The Distance With Scales

Color and cut out the pictures at the bottom of the page.
Then read each clue below.
Use the compass rose, map scale, and centimeter ruler
   to decide where each picture belongs.
Glue the picture in place.

1 cm = 1 mile

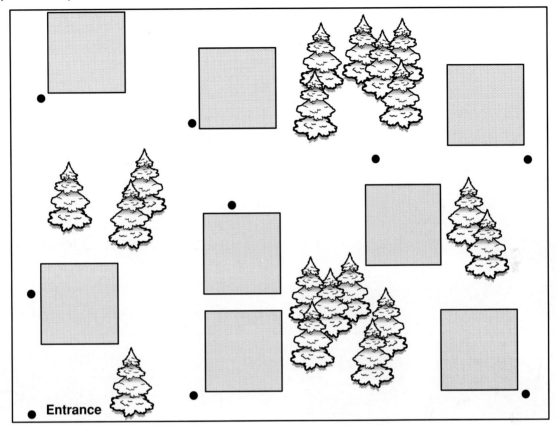

1. Grassy Meadow is 3 miles north of the entrance sign.

2. Lookout Cliff is 5 miles north of Grassy Meadow.

3. Wild River is 4 miles east of Lookout Cliff.

4. Spring Lake is 7 miles south of Wild River.

5. Dark Cavern is 9 miles east of Spring Lake.

6. The Grande Mountains are 6 miles north of Dark Cavern.

7. Green Forest is 4 miles west of the Grande Mountains.

8. The Ranger Station is 4 miles southwest of Green Forest.

Bonus Box: On the back of this page, write the names of two places on the map. Then write how many miles apart they are.

©The Education Center, Inc. • *Ready-to-Go Lessons* • TEC1116

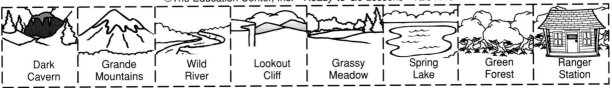

| Dark Cavern | Grande Mountains | Wild River | Lookout Cliff | Grassy Meadow | Spring Lake | Green Forest | Ranger Station |

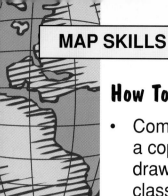

How To Extend The Lesson:

• Combine motivation and map scales with this incentive program. Enlarge a copy of Marty Mountaineer (shown below); color it and cut it out. Then draw a simple mountain shape on bulletin-board paper and display it on a classroom wall. Below the mountain, post the map scale 1 inch = 10 feet. Also post a sign that names the behavior you would like students to demonstrate, such as walking quietly in the halls. Then tell students that each time you see the featured behavior, you will move Marty ten feet up the mountain. If students behave especially well, have Marty climb an extra ten feet. Celebrate reaching the summit with a popcorn treat.

• Have students make a map of the classroom with this hands-on activity. Give each student a piece of half-inch graph paper, a ruler, and a pencil. Using a tape measure, determine the length and width of the classroom in feet. Have students draw the perimeter of the classroom on their papers, each square representing one foot. Then have students measure items in the room, such as desks, tables, and bookshelves. Instruct students to add the items to their maps, keeping them to scale.

• For a personal twist to learning about map scales, have students measure themselves. Using the scale 1 inch = 1 foot, have pairs of students measure each other from head to foot. Instruct each student to round her height to the nearest foot and draw a scaled-down version of herself. Below each picture, have the student copy and complete the following sentence: "[Name] would be ____ inches tall." Display the pictures under the caption "If A Foot Were An Inch..."

Way Out West

Send your youngsters time traveling with this community services lesson.

Skill: Identifying services of a community

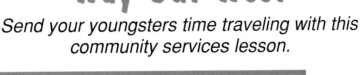

Estimated Lesson Time: 30 minutes

Teacher Preparation:
Duplicate page 299 for each student.

Materials:
1 copy of page 299 for each student
crayons
scissors
glue

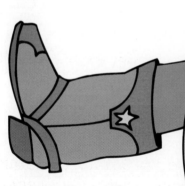

Background Information:
A community provides services to meet the needs and wants of its citizens. A community manages fire and police departments to keep citizens safe. The public works department provides clean water for citizens, treats waste water, and collects garbage. A community's health services might include hospitals and clinics. Transportation services provide citizens with public transportation, such as buses and trains. Public schools help citizens meet their need for an education. To enhance the lives of its citizens, communities provide parks, museums, and libraries.

Introducing The Lesson:

On the chalkboard, draw a large cactus, a horizon line, and some distant mountains (see the illustration). Invite students to imagine that they have been transported back in time to a Wild West settlement. Explain that the settlement has homes and stores that meet their needs for food, clothing, and shelter. Then tell students that their new community does not provide other services they might want. Ask students what safety and recreational services they would like their new community to have. Accept reasonable responses, such as police, hospitals, and parks.

Steps:

1. Explain to students that people benefit from living in a community because it provides many services for its citizens. Then share the Background Information on page 297.

2. Distribute a copy of page 299, crayons, glue, and scissors to each student. Next have a volunteer read aloud the directions at the top of the page. Then instruct each student to complete the page independently.

3. Challenge students to complete the Bonus Box activity.

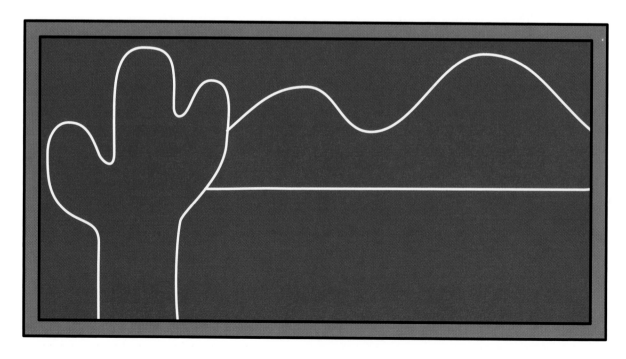

Name _____

Way Out West

Color and cut out the picture cards.
Read each service on the map.
Put a drop of glue on each •. Glue the matching picture in place.

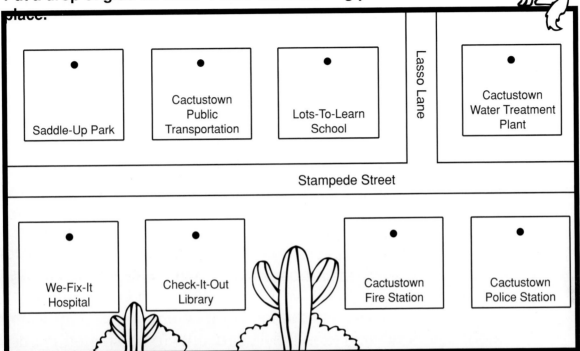

On the lines below, write the need that each service meets.

1. Saddle-Up Park _____

_____

2. Cactustown Public Transportation _____

_____

3. Lots-To-Learn School _____

_____

4. Cactustown Water Treatment Plant _____

_____

5. We-Fix-It Hospital _____

_____

6. Check-It-Out Library _____

_____

7. Cactustown Fire Station _____

_____

8. Cactustown Police Station _____

_____

How To Extend The Lesson:

- Put your community on display with this quilt activity. Have each child brainstorm the types of recreation in her community, such as swimming or roller-skating. Then instruct her to select a type of recreation and draw a picture of it on a nine-inch construction-paper square. Mount the completed squares on a length of bulletin-board paper to form a quilt. Use a marker to draw "stitches" around each square. Then display the quilt on a prominent wall and title it "Having Fun In Our Community!"

- Use this fun flip-book activity to explore the services of your community. To make a flip book, a student stacks two sheets of drawing paper; then holds the bottom piece in place and slides the top sheet upward to create two graduated layers. He folds both papers forward to create four graduated layers. Next the child staples the resulting booklet close to the fold. Each student titles the first layer "What My Community Provides," and then labels a layer for each of the following categories: Safety, Recreation, and Education (see the illustration). To complete the booklet project, a student writes two statements about each category on its corresponding page; then he illustrates the pages.

- This center idea reinforces students' reading skills and their understanding of community services. On different colored sentence strips, write a sentence about a community service in three different colors as shown below. Make each sentence self-checking by writing the numeral 1 on the back of each strip of the first sentence, the numeral 2 on the back of each strip of the second sentence, and so forth until each sentence has been programmed. Mix the strips together and place them in a large folder labeled "Community Mix-Up!" To complete the activity, the student reads each strip, arranges groups of three strips into sentences, and flips the strips to check her answers.

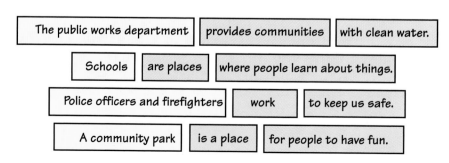

The public works department	provides communities	with clean water.
Schools	are places	where people learn about things.
Police officers and firefighters	work	to keep us safe.
A community park	is a place	for people to have fun.

Serve It Up!

*Serve up a hearty helping of goods and services
with this made-to-order lesson.*

Skill: Distinguishing between goods and services

Estimated Lesson Time: 35 minutes

Teacher Preparation:
Duplicate page 303 for each student.

Materials:
1 copy of page 303 for each student
1 rubber ball (or beanbag)
scissors
glue

Background Information:
In a community, people use goods and services
each day. *Goods* are items that people make or
grow, such as clothing and corn. *Services* are jobs
that you pay someone else to do for you, such as
car repairs and checkups with a doctor.

Introducing The Lesson:

Toss the rubber ball to a student. After the child catches the ball, have him name something bought from a store, such as bubble gum or shoes. Then have the student toss the ball back to you. Record the youngster's idea on the chalkboard under the heading "Store Items" (see the sample list). Continue in this manner until half of the students have named a store item. Then follow the same procedure with the other half of students, having each of them name an occupation, such as teaching or repairing cars. Record students' ideas on the chalkboard under the heading "Occupations" (see the sample list). Then explain that each word on the chalkboard is either a good or a service.

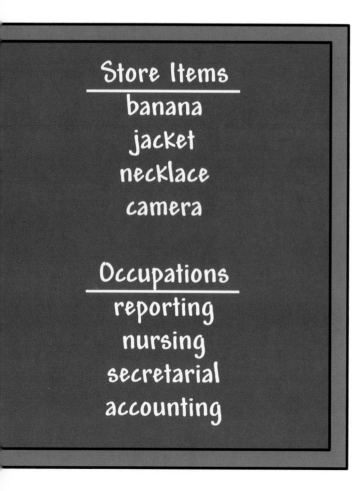

Store Items
banana
jacket
necklace
camera

Occupations
reporting
nursing
secretarial
accounting

Steps:

1. Share with students the Background Information on page 301.

2. Direct students to read the words on the chalkboard. Have them determine which column of words includes goods and which includes services. Change the "Store Items" heading to "Goods" and the "Occupations" heading to "Services." Then ask students how each good or service helps people in a community.

3. Distribute scissors, glue, and a copy of page 303 to each student. Ask a volunteer to read aloud the directions at the top of the page. Have each student complete the reproducible independently.

4. Challenge students to complete the Bonus Box activity.

Name ____________________ *Distinguishing between goods and services*

Serve It Up!

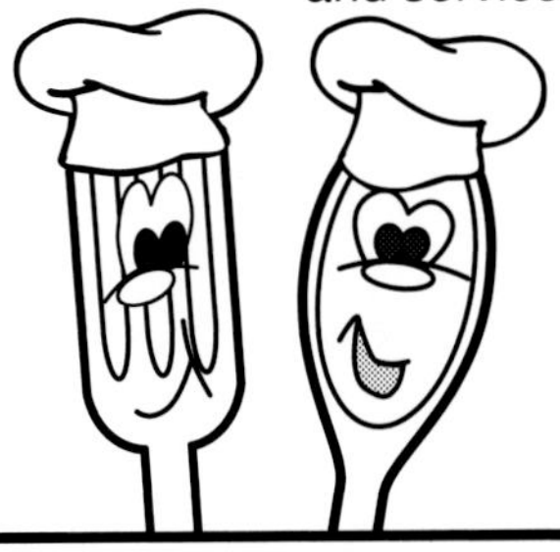

Read the words on the boxes.
Cut out each box and glue it on the matching menu page.
On each box, write your answer to the question.

Gourmet Goods Who provides each good?	**Scrumptious Services** What type of service does each worker provide?

Bonus Box: On the back of this sheet, write three more goods and three more services.

postal worker	car	doctor	lifeguard	books	fruit	farmer	shoes

How To Extend The Lesson:

- Show students several goods that they use daily, such as a toothbrush, a comb, food, a pencil, and a book. Have youngsters orally share why each good is important to them.

- Brainstorm with students a list of services provided in your school (teaching, cleaning, cooking). Record students' ideas on the chalkboard. Under your students' direction, write the name of each person who does the job next to the service. Then have each student write a thank-you note to a different school helper. Direct her to include in the note the goods and services the employee provides and how the worker helps the school community.

- Put goods and services in the spotlight with this art activity. Divide the class into small groups. Have each group think of a place in which both goods and services are provided, such as a grocery store or a department store. Then give each group a length of bulletin-board paper. Have the group write goods and services associated with its place in the middle of the paper. Direct the group to draw a box around the lists and write the name of the location underneath it. Next have the group draw pictures around the box of the goods and services to create an eye-catching border. Display the completed projects around your classroom, and encourage youngsters to check out the many goods and services provided in the different locations.

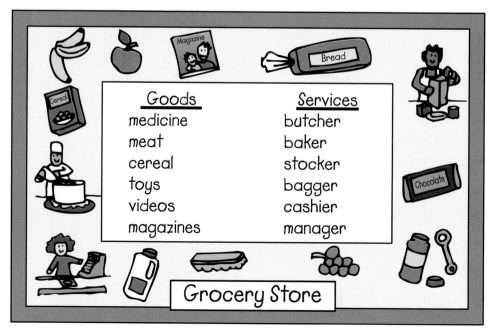

Goods	Services
medicine	butcher
meat	baker
cereal	stocker
toys	bagger
videos	cashier
magazines	manager

Grocery Store

Monkeying Around With Labor

Swing into a study of specialization and division of labor with this "ap-peel-ing" lesson!

Skill: Applying an understanding of specialization and division of labor

Estimated Lesson Time: 40 minutes

Teacher Preparation:
Duplicate page 307 onto white construction paper for each student, plus one extra.

Materials:
1 white construction-paper copy of page 307 for each student, plus one extra
1 set of crayons for each group
1 pair of scissors for each group
glue for each group

Background Information:
In communities people share their learning and work to complete big jobs. People do different jobs to save time. *Division of labor* is the breakdown of a whole job into parts. It is a faster way to make goods. *Specialization* means a person focuses on a certain part of a job.

Introducing The Lesson:

Draw an outline of a car on the chalkboard (see the example below). As students name different parts of a car, label each part on the car's outline. Ask students how they think the parts are put together to make a car. Explain that cars are built in factories using division of labor and specialization.

Steps:

1. Share with students the Background Information on page 305. Explain to students that they will use division of labor and specialization to create decorated gift boxes.

2. Divide the class into groups of four students. Give each group four construction-paper copies of page 307, scissors, crayons, and glue. Have a student volunteer read aloud the directions on a copy of page 307. Ask youngsters to name the tasks necessary to complete the gift box (decorating, cutting, folding, gluing).

3. Using the extra copy of page 307, demonstrate for students how to fold and glue a gift box.

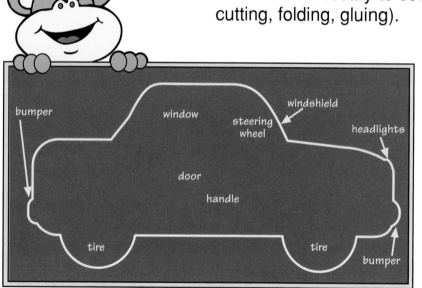

4. Assign one student in each group a specialized task (decorating, cutting, folding, gluing) to be completed for each box. Explain that making these job assignments is an example of division of labor. Remind students to work on each box quickly and neatly. Then direct each group to use the patterns and materials to assemble four gift boxes.

5. After students have finished their projects, have each youngster tell about his experience. Discuss with students how division of labor and specializing in a particular task helped to finish the project faster or better.

Directions:

1. Decorate each pattern as desired.
2. Cut out the box and lid patterns.
3. Fold the patterns on the dotted lines.
4. Glue the tabs to the inside of the box and lid patterns.

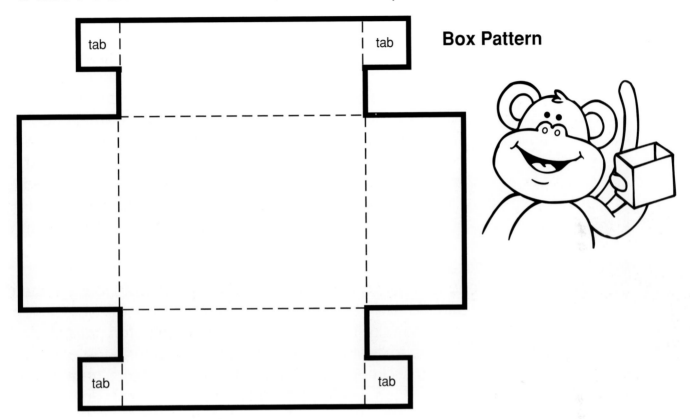

Box Pattern

tab   tab

tab   tab

Lid Pattern

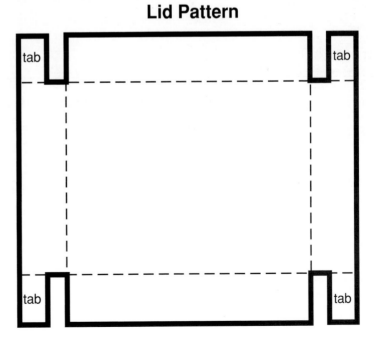

tab   tab

tab   tab

ECONOMICS

How To Extend The Lesson:

- Have youngsters practice division of labor by creating candy trucks. Divide your class into teams of four students. Tell students that each group will be completing four candy trucks. To create a candy truck, one student breaks a large graham cracker into four smaller pieces. Then he uses a knife to

spread a thick layer of frosting on one piece. The next child attaches four Lifesavers® candies to the frosting on the cracker for the wheels (see the illustration). The third student frosts the bottom of a caramel cube and attaches it to the top of the graham cracker for a cab. The last child carefully places the edible vehicle in a resealable plastic bag. Have the groups repeat the procedure until each child has a candy truck.

- Help an overworked hen by applying an understanding of specialization! Read aloud *The Little Red Hen* by Paul Galdone (Houghton Mifflin Company, 1985). Tell students that because the hen did everything to make the flour, the least her friends could do is make the cake! After sharing the story, direct youngsters to list the tasks involved in preparing the cake (gathering sticks, building a fire, mixing a cake). Then ask students which job would best suit each animal (cat, dog, mouse). Have students share their choices and reasons for them. If desired, delve deeper into specialization by having pairs of students write an advertisement for a job mentioned in the story.

I need a doctor to give me drugs to sleep during surgery. (*anesthesiologist*)

I need to have my heart checked. (*cardiologist*)

I am having trouble with my skin. (*dermatologist*)

I need to have my blood checked. (*hematologist*)

I am having trouble with my nervous system. (*neurologist*)

Something is wrong with my eyes. (*ophthalmologist*)

My baby is sick. (*pediatrician*)

I need a doctor to read my X ray. (*radiologist*)

- Illustrate the concept of specialization by taking a closer look at the medical profession. In advance, create a list of specialist-related clues such as, "I am having trouble with my heart. Which doctor should I see?" Post a list of medical specialists that correspond with the clues. Then read each clue about doctors and enlist students' help in matching it to the corresponding specialist. Encourage each youngster to find out more about a medical specialty that interests her.

Applying an understanding of specialization and division of labor

Producer Or Consumer?

Students discover information about consumers and producers with this hands-on activity.

Skill: Understanding that a producer is a consumer

Estimated Lesson Time: 30 minutes

Teacher Preparation:
Duplicate page 311 onto light-colored construction paper for each student.

Materials:
4 chairs
1 construction-paper copy of
    page 311 for each student
1 brad for each student
scissors
crayons
writing paper

Background Information:
A *producer* is a person who makes goods or provides a service. A taxi driver, a baker, and a teacher are all producers. A *consumer* is a person who uses goods or services. A person who pays for a taxi ride or buys bread is a consumer. When a producer spends the money he earns, he is a consumer too. For example, a taxi driver (a producer) is a consumer when he pays for fuel. The money goes from consumer to producer and back again.

Introducing The Lesson:

Arrange four chairs to represent a car (see the illustration below). Then sit in the driver's seat and tell students to imagine that you are a taxi driver. Pretend to start the engine and ask if anyone needs a ride. Select two volunteers to sit in the backseat and ask them where they need to go. After a few moments of driving, apply the brakes and tell the passengers the amount of their fare. Have students pretend to pay you before they return to their seats. Next, as you drive off, announce that your taxi needs fuel and you are driving to a gas station. Ask for a volunteer to fill your taxi's tank. Once the tank is full, ask her how much you owe and pretend to pay her. Then have her return to her seat.

Steps:

1. Explain to students that you have just acted as a producer and a consumer. Then share the Background Information on page 309 with students. Ask students for other examples of a person who is both a producer and a consumer.

2. Distribute a copy of page 311 and a brad to each student. Have students color and cut out the patterns. Instruct students to assemble the wheel by inserting the brad first through the wheel and then through each hole of the strips.

3. Ask a student volunteer to read aloud the first example on the wheel. Have students determine if the baker in this situation is a producer or a consumer. Confirm the correct response and have each student rotate her corresponding strip to align behind the example. Continue in this manner until all examples have been read and identified.

4. Finally, on a sheet of writing paper, have each student list three situations when a doctor is a producer (for example: *gives shots, gives physical examinations, and checks eyes*). Then have the student list five situations when a doctor is a consumer (for example: *buys office supplies, pays power bills, and buys equipment*).

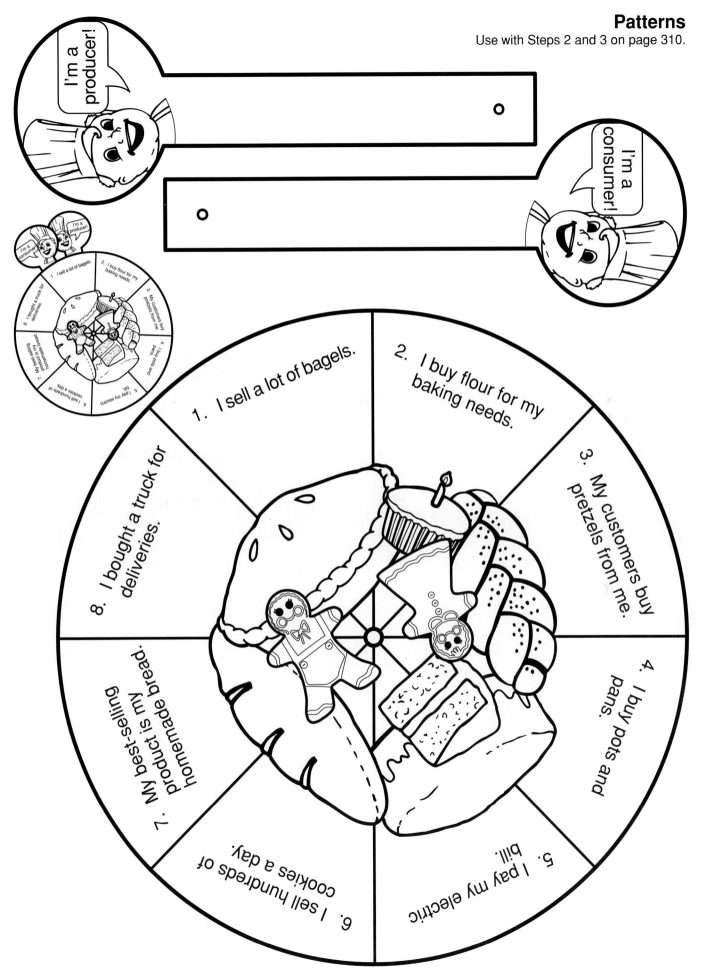

I'm a producer!

I'm a consumer!

1. I sell a lot of bagels.

2. I buy flour for my baking needs.

3. My customers buy pretzels from me.

4. I buy pots and pans.

5. I pay my electric bill.

6. I sell hundreds of cookies a day.

7. My best-selling product is my homemade bread.

8. I bought a truck for deliveries.

How To Extend The Lesson:

- Have each student construct a collage of consumers and producers. For each student, cut a large, construction-paper *C* and *P* or, if desired, have students make their own. Provide students with discarded magazines and instruct each student to glue pictures of consumers on the *C* and pictures of producers on the *P*. Then have each student attach a self-adhesive star on each producer that is also a consumer.

- Explore the travels of a dollar bill in the book *The Go-Around Dollar* by Barbara Johnston Adams (Simon & Schuster Books For Young Readers, 1992). After reading the book aloud, enlist students' help in creating a chart that shows the exchanges the dollar encounters. Label the people involved in the exchanges as consumers or producers.

- This center game reinforces memory practice *and* student understanding of consumers and producers. Label index cards as shown below; then place the cards in a center. To play the game, two students shuffle the cards and place them facedown. Then the first player turns over two cards. If the two cards have corresponding information, the player keeps the cards and takes another turn. If the cards do not match, the player turns the two cards facedown and the other player takes a turn. The game is over when all cards have been taken. The player with the most cards wins!

mechanic repairs cars | mechanic producer

mechanic buys tools | mechanic consumer

teacher teaches children | teacher producer

teacher buys supplies | teacher consumer

dog groomer bathes dogs | dog groomer producer

dog groomer buys dog shampoo | dog groomer consumer

chef cooks for people | chef producer

chef pays for food deliveries | chef consumer

Place-Value Patterns

Use with "Regrouping Rally" on page 93 and the second extension activity on page 104.

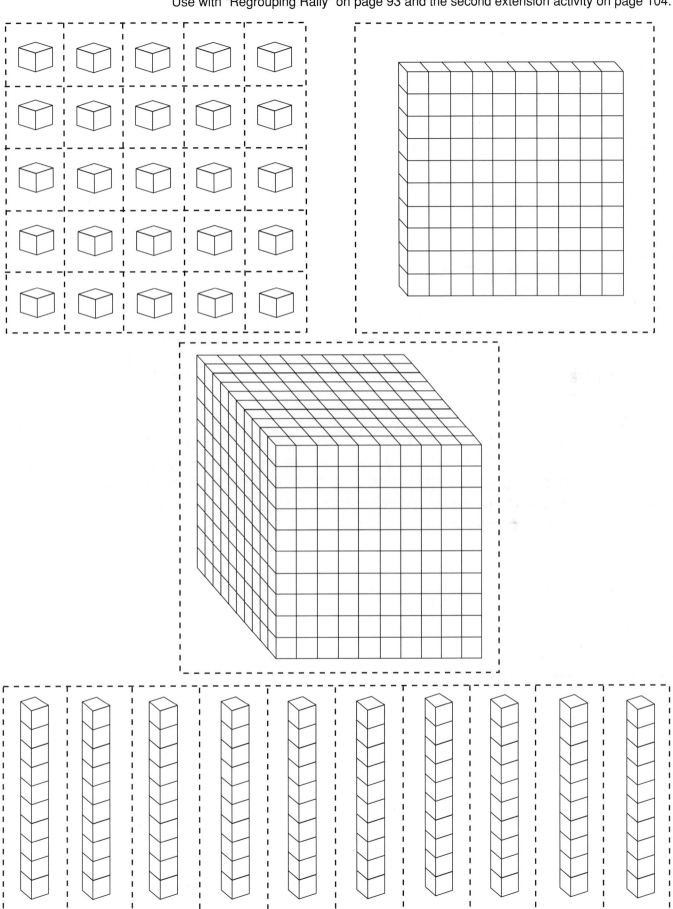

Coin Patterns

Use with the third extension activity on page 100.

Fraction Circles

Use with "Freewheeling Fractions" on page 113 and the second extension activity on page 116.

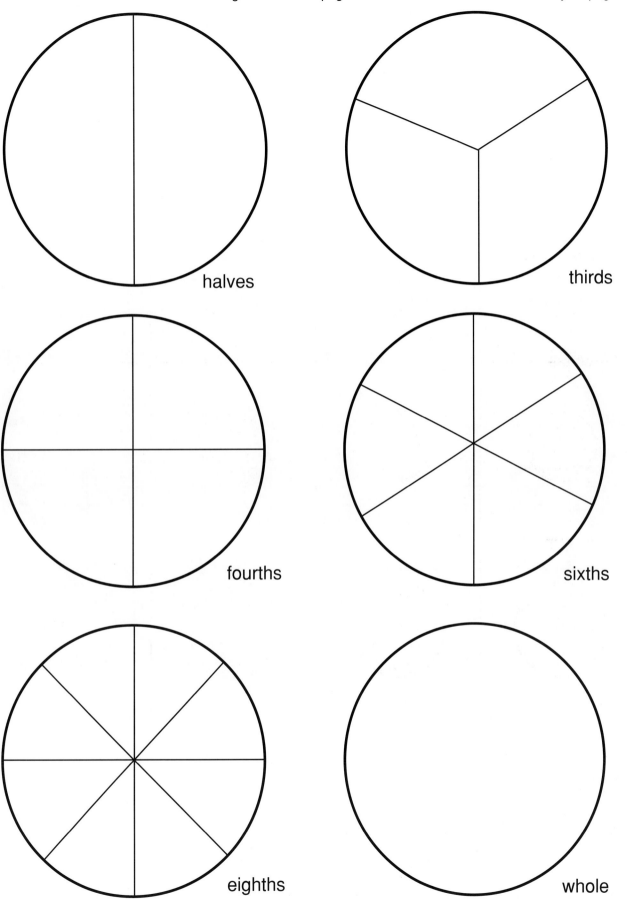

halves

thirds

fourths

sixths

eighths

whole

Analog Clock Pattern

Use with "Wally's Watch" on page 157 and "From Time To Time" on page 161.

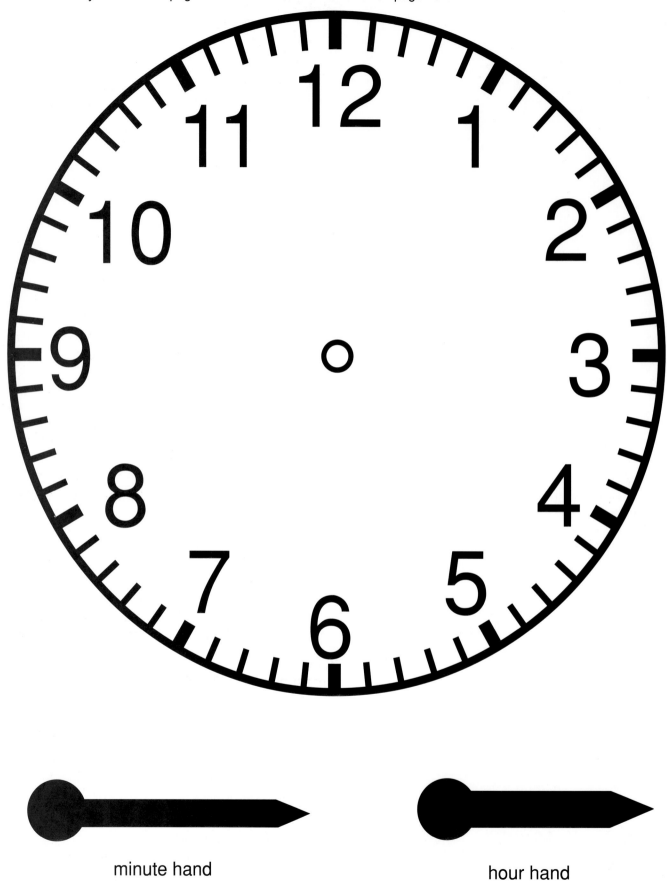

minute hand

hour hand

Answer Keys

Page 7

smart	enclose
smear	engine
smile	enjoy
smoke	enough
smudge	enter

grape	class
great	clever
grill	climb
growl	cloud
grudge	club

black
blend
blind
blow
blush

Page 15

1. Dr. = Doctor
2. Jr. = Junior
3. U.S.A. = United States of America
4. Tues. = Tuesday
5. Jan. = January
6. 1st = first
7. E.R. = Emergency Room
8. St. = Street
9. Rd. = Road
10. 3rd = third

Page 23

The word listed first by each number should be circled on the student's paper.

1. sum, some
2. sun, son
3. write, right
4. bear, bare
5. deer, dear
6. flower, flour
7. wood, would
8. nose, knows
9. hare, hair

Page 95

1. 44 (red)
2. 52 (red)
3. 38 (blue)
4. 72 (red)
5. 54 (red)
6. 77 (blue)
7. 56 (red)
8. 40 (red)
9. 69 (blue)
10. 81 (red)
11. 91 (red)
12. 78 (blue)
13. 94 (red)
14. 61 (red)
15. 94 (blue)

Page 99

Joe's Snack Attack

Joe has 90¢.
He bought a sno-cone.
How much money is left?

$$\begin{array}{r} \overset{8\ 1}{\cancel{9}\cancel{0}} \\ -\ 38 \\ \hline 52\,¢ \end{array}$$

Then Joe bought some peanuts.
How much money is left?

$$\begin{array}{r} \overset{4\ 1}{\cancel{5}\cancel{2}} \\ -\ 25 \\ \hline 27\,¢ \end{array}$$

Joe also bought popcorn.
How much money is left?

$$\begin{array}{r} \overset{1\ 1}{\cancel{2}\cancel{7}} \\ -\ 19 \\ \hline 8\,¢ \end{array}$$

What could Joe buy with the money left over?

hard candy

Jane's Snack Attack

Jane has 90¢.
She bought cotton candy.
How much money is left?

$$\begin{array}{r} \overset{8\ 1}{\cancel{9}\cancel{0}} \\ -\ 48 \\ \hline 42\,¢ \end{array}$$

Then Jane bought a lollipop.
How much money is left?

$$\begin{array}{r} \overset{3\ 1}{\cancel{4}\cancel{2}} \\ -\ 27 \\ \hline 15\,¢ \end{array}$$

Jane also bought a pickle.
How much money is left?

$$\begin{array}{r} 15 \\ -\ 12 \\ \hline 3\,¢ \end{array}$$

What could Jane buy with the money left over?

nothing

Page 103

4, 3, 6, 2

largest number—6,432
smallest number—2,346
smallest numeral in tens place—answers will vary, but the 2 must be in the tens place
largest numeral in hundreds place—answers will vary, but the 6 must be in the hundreds place

2, 9, 0, 6

largest number—9,620
smallest number—269
smallest numeral in tens place—answers will vary, but the 0 must be in the tens place
largest numeral in hundreds place—answers will vary, but the 9 must be in the hundreds place

7, 8, 1, 5

largest number—8,751
smallest number—1,578
smallest numeral in tens place—answers will vary, but the 1 must be in the tens place
largest numeral in hundreds place—answers will vary, but the 8 must be in the hundreds place

3, 0, 8, 4

largest number—8,430
smallest number—348
smallest numeral in tens place—answers will vary, but the 0 must be in the tens place
largest numeral in hundreds place—answers will vary, but the 8 must be in the hundreds place

2, 5, 1, 7

largest number—7,521
smallest number—1,257
smallest numeral in tens place—answers will vary, but the 1 must be in the tens place
largest numeral in hundreds place—answers will vary, but the 7 must be in the hundreds place

Page 111

baseball bat
$\frac{1}{2}$ off = $8.00   sale price = $8.00

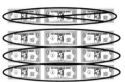

glove
$\frac{1}{4}$ off = $2.00   sale price = $6.00

bowling ball
$\frac{1}{4}$ off = $3.00   sale price = $9.00

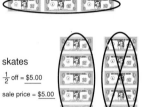

football
$\frac{1}{3}$ off = $3.00   sale price = $6.00

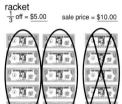

racket
$\frac{1}{3}$ off = $5.00   sale price = $10.00

skates
$\frac{1}{2}$ off = $5.00

sale price = $5.00

Page 115

1. 1/2 = **2**/4
2. 1/4 = **2**/8
3. 1/3 = **2**/6
4. 1/2 = **3**/6
5. 1/2 = **4**/8
6. 2/4 = **4**/8
7. 2/3 = **4**/6
8. 3/4 = **6**/8

Page 139

1. add   4 + 2 + 2 = 8
2. subtract   9 − 4 = 5
3. add   5 + 4 + 7 + 3 = 19
4. add   11 + 14 = 25
5. subtract   84 − 79 = 5
6. subtract   9 − 5 = 4
7. subtract   67 − 35 = 32
8. add   4 + 6 + 3 = 13

Page 155

1. 30°F
2. 66°F
3. 36°F
4. 42°F
5. 78°F
6. 62°F
7. 26°F
8. 56°F

Page 159

1. The real time is **2:15**.
   Wally's watch would show **2:30**.

2. The real time is **5:30**.
   Wally's watch would show **5:45**.

3. The real time is **9:00**.
   Wally's watch would show **9:15**.

4. The real time is **7:15**.
   Wally's watch would show **7:30**.

5. The real time is **1:45**.
   Wally's watch would show **2:00**.

6. The real time is **11:30**.
   Wally's watch would show **11:45**.

7. The real time is **10:00**.
   Wally's watch would show **10:15**.

8. The real time is **4:45**.
   Wally's watch would show **5:00**.

Page 183

1. anteater   6. bee
2. duck   7. bat
3. spider   8. eagle
4. snake   9. frog
5. shark   10. elephant

Page 199

(Answers will vary.)
1. There are changes in size and shape.
   Yes.
   It is a physical change.
2. There are changes in size, shape, color, texture, and substance.
   No.
   It is a chemical change.
3. There are changes in size and shape.
   Yes.
   It is a physical change.
4. There are changes in color and substance.
   No.
   It is a chemical change.
5. There are changes in color.
   Yes.
   It is a physical change.

Page 207

(The order of answers in each category may vary.)

Transparent: clean water, clear glass, plastic wrap, clean air

Translucent: waxed paper, paper towel, tissue paper, cloud

Opaque: cardboard, aluminum foil, wood, black poster board

Page 215

(The order of answers in each category may vary.)

Natural Heat Sources: lightning, sun, geyser, volcano

Man-Made Heat Sources: oven, lightbulb, matches, toaster

Page 247

(Answers may vary.)

1. The police officer keeps people a safe distance from the fire.
2. The police officer keeps people out of the way so the firefighters can do their job.
3. The firefighters don't have to take time to apply first aid to victims because the EMTs will do it.
4. The police officer keeps people out of the way so the EMTs can do their job.
5. The firefighters bring injured people out of the building so the EMTs can work in safety.

Bonus Box: (Answers may vary.) Citizens can help by staying out of the way of the rescuers.

Page 255

(Answers may vary.)

1. Keep your dog on a leash.
2. Ride your bicycle on the right-hand side of the road.
3. Bag yard clippings. Do not burn trash within the city limits.
4. Do not leave open barrels or containers in your yard.
5. Do not let poison oak or poison ivy grow in your yard.
6. Put litter in its proper container.
7. Wear a helmet when in-line skating.

Page 267

Everglades

These marshlands, found in Florida, have plains of grass and trees.

You'll find a variety of wildlife here including alligators, cougars, manatees, and many birds.

Statue of Liberty

It's a long way to the top! From its feet to the tip of its torch, this sculpture is over 150 feet high.

What a popular place! Each year about two million people visit this statue of a robed woman.

Grand Canyon

Carved by the Colorado River, this hole in the ground is over one mile deep in places.

At sunset the red and brown layers in this canyon's walls are a beautiful sight.

Mount Rushmore

This huge sculpture of four U.S. presidents is found in the Black Hills of South Dakota.

These four faces are George Washington, Thomas Jefferson, Theodore Roosevelt, and Abraham Lincoln.

Page 275

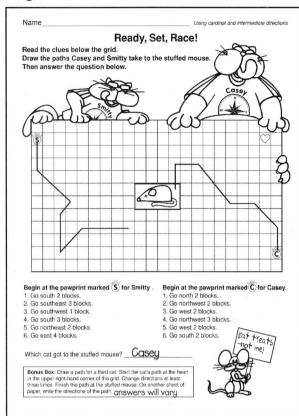

Bonus Box: Answers will vary.

Page 279

1. D3
2. E1
3. B4
4. C1
5. E4
6. C3
7. A4
8. B5
9. video (Answers may vary.)
10. A1

Bonus Box: fuel at D5 or repairs at E2

Page 283

1. symbols
2. 4
3. apples
4. 4
5. apples
6. corn, peanuts
7. peanuts
8. cotton, peanuts, apples
9. peanuts
10. corn; Corn is the product that is grown the least.

Bonus Box: (Answers will vary.) cotton picker, peanut butter producer, apple juice producer

Page 287

1. B
2. H
3. C
4. J
5. A
6. F
7. G
8. E
9. D
10. I

1. harbor
2. island
3. gulf

Bonus Box: (Answers will vary.)

1. A peninsula has water on three sides and an island is completely surrounded by water.
2. A gulf is larger than a bay.

Page 288
Bird's-Eye View

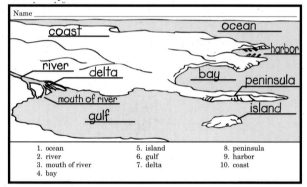

1. ocean
2. river
3. mouth of river
4. bay
5. island
6. gulf
7. delta
8. peninsula
9. harbor
10. coast

Page 291

1. Atlantic Ocean
2. Indian Ocean
3. Antarctica
4. Asia
5. South America

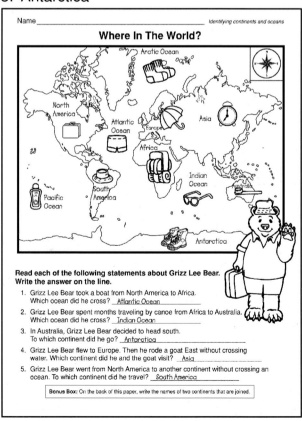

Bonus Box: North America and South America **or** Europe and Asia **or** Africa and Asia